PENGUIN BOOKS

CELESTIAL PASSENGERS

The daughter of a British army officer, Margaret Sachs has had the good fortune to live in such varied countries as Malaysia, Yugoslavia, Germany, and Norway. After finishing her education in England, she was employed at a London publishing house and then moved to Rome, where she worked as an assistant to two writers, Eugene Walter and Muriel Spark. Margaret Sachs now lives in California with her husband, a motion-picture director, and their five cats. *Celestial Passengers* is her first book.

Ernest Jahn is an investigator for the National Investigations Committee on Aerial Phenomena (NICAP). He is also an electronics specialist for the New York Telephone Company. He lives on Staten Island, New York, with his wife and two children.

Celestial Passengers

UFO'S
AND SPACE TRAVEL

BY

Margaret Sachs

WITH

Ernest Jahn

PENGUIN BOOKS

Penguin Books Ltd, Harmondsworth,
Middlesex, England
Penguin Books, 625 Madison Avenue,
New York, New York 10022, U.S.A.
Penguin Books Australia Ltd, Ringwood,
Victoria, Australia
Penguin Books Canada Limited, 2801 John Street,
Markham, Ontario, Canada L3R 1B4
Penguin Books (N.Z.) Ltd, 182–190 Wairau Road,
Auckland 10, New Zealand

First published 1977
Reprinted 1978 (twice)

LIBRARY OF CONGRESS CATALOGING IN PUBLICATION DATA
Sachs, Margaret.
Celestial passengers.
1. Flying saucers. I. Jahn, Ernest, joint author.
II. Title.
TL789.S15   001.9′42   77-9023
ISBN 0 14 00.4483 3

Printed in the United States of America by
Offset Paperback Mfrs., Inc., Dallas, Pennsylvania
Set in Linotype Caledonia

The cartoons from *B.C.* by Johnny Hart are reprinted by
permission of John Hart and Field Enterprises, Inc.

To Florence
for the many hours of moral support and assistance,
and to Bill
for his direction and guidance

Contents

PART TWO
EXTRATERRESTRIAL LIFE

PART THREE
A WATCHFUL EYE ON CELESTIAL OBJECTS

PART FOUR
UFO CASE HISTORIES

Contents

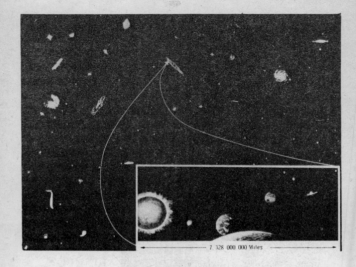

7,328,000,000 Miles

THE UNIVERSE

The Earth is a minor planet circling around an average star in a galaxy of 100 billion stars which occupies a pinpoint of space among untold billions of galaxies in the universe.

The solar system is 7 billion, 328 million miles in diameter, taking up a speck of space about two-thirds of the way out from the center of the Milky Way, which is about 100,000 light years across. A light year is the distance traveled at the speed of light—186,000 miles a second—in one year.
(Courtesy NASA)

ACKNOWLEDGMENTS

We wish to express our gratitude to all who made this book possible by their generous contributions of material and illustrations.

We are deeply grateful to Albert Chop, Dr. Robert Jastrow, John L. Acuff, Jr., Les Gaver, Marcia S. Smith, Dan McHugh, Loren Abdulezer, John A. O'Keefe, Peter Tompkins, Donn Davison, Nicholas Vreeland, and to the staff of Wagner College Planetarium, Staten Island.

Special acknowledgment is made to the National Aeronautics and Space Administration, the National Space Institute, and the Polytechnic Institute of New York.

Our special thanks to the National Investigations Committee on Aerial Phenomena for permission to publish case histories from their files which are included in Chapters 15 through 23, and 26.

The information in Chapter 23 is taken from *Spinoff 1976* by Neil P. Ruzic, courtesy of the National Space Institute and the Technical Division of the National Aeronautics and Space Administration.

And lastly we wish to thank all those who took the time to make statements to us and permitted us to quote their opinions in this book.

PREFACE

"Don't laugh, but I think I'm looking at a UFO!" I turned around and looked across the Howard Johnson's parking lot to see my husband, Bill, approaching the car, his eyes fixed on a point about 40 degrees above the distant horizon.

My skepticism arose from the fact that we were returning to New York City from Washington, D.C., after a painstaking month of research at the National Archives. We had been preparing materials for *The Force Beyond*, a motion picture Bill was directing, which dealt with various unsolved mysteries, UFO's in particular. During the enthusiasm of that month we had seen countless "UFO's" that within seconds became discernible as mere mortal aircraft. This was just another false alarm, I thought. Besides, no one has the good fortune to see a UFO when looking for one.

As Bill walked up and got into the car beside me, I turned forward and looked through the windshield to scan the sky. Then I saw it, too. An elliptical object hung there motionless between us and the setting sun. Oddly, the object was tilted at a 45-degree angle to the horizon and emitted a brilliant glow. At first we thought that it was reflecting the sunlight, but then we realized that this was impossible since the sun was on the other side of the object. "Damn it! There's no film in the camera," said Bill. He ran back into the Howard Johnson's hoping that they sold film, but luck was against us. The camera lay useless on the seat.

We sat in the car for about ten minutes watching that strange magnesiumlike glow. It did not budge. It was getting late and we still had a long drive ahead of us. We decided it was time to continue on our journey. Just as Bill put the key in the ignition, we noticed that the object was moving. It was descending at a slow, steady speed. We watched, fascinated, until it was blocked from our vision by a line of tall trees a few hundred yards in front of us. We waited for a few moments to see if the object would reappear, but it did not. We gave up and continued on our journey up the New Jersey Turnpike.

During our stay in Washington, D.C., we had visited the headquarters of the National Investigations Committee on Aerial Phenomena. There we had been given the name of their New York investigator, Ernest Jahn, who might, suggested NICAP's director, be able to assist us on the UFO section of the film. That evening, when we arrived back at our apartment in New York, Bill called Ernie. After introducing himself and explaining the project we were working on, Bill told him about the puzzling object we had seen. Ernie promised to follow up with inquiries. Several days later he called us back with confirmation. In the area of New Jersey over which we had seen the object there had been several close-up sightings of metallic disks. Unfortunately, however, none of the reports was firsthand and Ernie was never able to trace down the original witnesses.

The film project proceeded and Ernie became totally involved, arranging for interviews with police officers and local officials as well as appearing in the film himself. After the commotion and chaos of shooting the film had ended and we had all settled down to a more serene routine, we planned to get together with Ernie and his wife, Florence, for a purely social evening. After dinner at their home on Staten Island we sat around the crackling fire on a cold January evening while Ernie told us of the peculiar cases he had been involved in during his time as New York investigator for NICAP. These were not the second- or thirdhand stories repeated in a hundred UFO publications. These were firsthand, unpublished accounts of genuine UFO sightings in which every avenue had been explored in vain to try to find an explanation. So caught up were we that none of us noticed the clock hands creeping around to the early morning hours. As the blackness of the night outside began to fade, Bill and I found ourselves saying, over and over again, "You should write a book!"

But Ernie's schedule was already overflowing, his days kept busy by his position as an electronics specialist for the New York Telephone Company, his evenings and weekends occupied by his activities for NICAP. "I've often thought of writing a book," he said, "but it would take me a few hundred years." Since my work on the film was finished, Bill immediately volunteered my services!

The following weekend we returned to Ernie's house equipped with tape recorder and notebooks. We were determined not to hack out another sensationalist publication where statements are unsubstantiated and often just repetition of other authors' works. We wanted to present case histories of UFO sightings that are reliable either because Ernie himself had investigated them or because they were verified by other NICAP investigators. In this sense we hope that this book will stand out from the countless "UFO books" whose sole aim is to exploit the subject and titillate the reader's mind with far-fetched, unauthenticated stories. It is true that many of the strongest cases on file do not have sensational public appeal, but we have chosen an interesting cross section that displays as many different aspects as possible of the UFO phenomenon. UFO's have been observed by people from all walks of life: technically trained observers, such as military and civilian pilots, radar controllers, scientists, and astronauts, and responsible persons, such as judges, civil defense officials, professors, lawyers, and clergymen, as well as hard-headed "ordinary" citizens. As Captain Eddie Rickenbacker said, "Flying saucers are real. Too many good men have seen them, that don't have hallucinations."

We must point out, though, that UFO means "unidentified flying object." It does not mean flying saucer, extraterrestrial spacecraft, or any other popular notion of the phenomenon. Whether UFO's are in fact spacecraft we do not know. That they exist, we do know. We do believe that there is some kind of unexplained phenomenon that cannot be explained in terms of psychological aberrations, astronomic events, or conventional aircraft.

But the title of this book does not refer merely to UFO's. With the help and advice of astronauts, scientists, politicians, and other qualified people, many of whom contributed a great deal of material, we have tried to present an overall picture of all the celestial passengers of our universe, unknown and known. Although the combination of subjects might seem unusual to some, what would a discussion on aerial phenomena be, after all, without a look at one of the most amazing aerial events of our time, our very own space program?

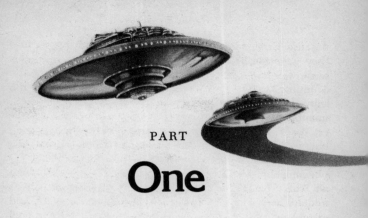

PART

One

WE DON'T KNOW
EVERYTHING YET

· 1 ·

STRANGE THINGS
ARE HAPPENING

Is your curiosity tormented by unsolved mysteries? Do you wonder if there are physical laws other than those established by modern science? Is your sense of security troubled by the idea that the human race could be a primitive tribe in a universe of far more sophisticated and advanced civilizations? Do you deny that mankind has achieved the limits of his growth and must now face a bleak future of increased austerity in a dying world? If your answers to these questions are "no," then do not read this book.

Throughout history man has constantly made new discoveries that altered his previous conceptions. It is naive to contend that we today have reached the zenith of understanding and that new discoveries will occur only within the perimeters of our established scientific knowledge. The great geneticist and biometrician, J. B. S. Haldane, said that "the universe is not only queerer than we imagine, it is queerer than we *can* imagine." The endless mysteries that puzzle scientists and boggle the minds of those who seek knowledge lend support to that statement.

Our knowledge of the origin of the physical world we live in is pitifully small. How did the planetary systems, the stellar systems, and the galactic systems form? Is the universe of infinite age or did it have a beginning and will it have an end? Theories abound, but there is no definitive answer to these questions. We have sent probes to other planets and although man himself has set foot on the moon, he still cannot define its origin. Studies of lunar samples indicate that the moon was not part of the planet Earth as was once suspected.

Here on Earth the mystery of evolution remains unsolved. Darwin's theory on the origin of species is widely accepted, but there are many who cannot accept the thought that man descended from the ape. While their rejection of the theory may be ascribed to religious prejudice, the missing link between the ape and upright Homo sapiens remains unidentified.

Did a superior race exist on this planet before the great flood? Tales of Atlantis and Mu bear witness to the existence of great civilizations long before that of classic Greece. Plato described Atlantis as located beyond "the Pillars of Hercules," now known as the Straits of Gibraltar, which stand like gigantic natural pillars at the entrance to the Mediterranean. The lost continent submerged beneath the Atlantic Ocean was considered mere legend, however. In 1940 Edgar Cayce, the American clairvoyant,

predicted that Atlantis would rise in 1968 off the coast of Bimini in the Bahamas. In perfect accordance with his prediction, fishermen diving for lobsters there in 1968 saw gigantic blocks of stone protruding two feet above the surface of the shifting sand. It seemed that Atlantis had risen. Today exploration teams are finding more structures in that part of the ocean. Their work slowed down by the expense and difficulty of underwater excavation, they persevere in their attempts to analyse and identify these great slabs, whose astonishingly precise jointing is identical to that of the mysterious Pyramid of Cheops in Egypt.

The unearthing of sophisticated artifacts and ancient literature from all over the world suggests that the development of modern science during the past few centuries may simply be the rediscovery of ancient accomplishments. There is evidence that antediluvian races may have possessed knowledge of dry cell batteries, flying craft, the atom bomb, and many other inventions for which our present day civilization has taken credit. The great megalithic landmarks in the lands bordering on the Atlantic Ocean incorporate in their structures mathematical and astronomical information that was not rediscovered until thousands of years after their erection. What ancient intelligence conceived and designed the pyramids of Egypt and Central America, Stonehenge, and the prehistoric earthworks in southwestern England known as the Somerset Zodiac, a grand scale map of the stars recognizable only from the air? What is the purpose of the colossal geometric designs and drawings that can be seen from the air to fill thousands and thousands of acres of the desert plateaus of Nasca in Peru? How did the Mayas of Central America know about stars and planets that cannot be seen with the naked eye and have only been discovered in recent times through the use of highly developed observational equipment? Why did their calendar, which computed the solar year to the closest figure reached by any calendar outside of our contemporary one, also include a calendar of the Venutian solar year? Is it only coincidence that the Mayan civilization appeared at about the time of the supposed submergence of Atlantis? Is the striking similarity of the Mayan pyramids to those of Egypt also a coincidence? Unfortunately, many of these questions remain unanswered because the religious zeal of the early Spanish conquerors destroyed the records of this great civilization as the instruments of paganism. The little hieroglyphic writing that remains is so complex that most of it remains undeciphered to date.

The Atlantic Ocean holds other secrets, secrets that affect mankind today. One example is the Bermuda Triangle, extending northeast from Florida to Bermuda, then south to a point just past Puerto Rico, then northwest through the Bahamas and back to Florida. In this heavily traveled area ships, submarines, small boats, and aircraft disappear at an alarming rate. Some researchers claim as many as fifty losses a year, though more conservative estimates place the figure at a total of just over seventy to date. Most of the craft have left no floating wreckage, oil slicks, lifeboats, or bodies, either in the sea or washed up on neighboring shores. Very rarely is any message of impending danger sent out. Pilots and sea captains frequently report compass deviations while traversing this area, and these magnetic disturbances are often accompanied by the phenomenon known as "white water." Not only the surface of the ocean, but the sky, too, turns a milky white, so that there is no horizon visible, no division between sea and sky. This spot is also the scene of frequent sightings of UFO's and strange moving lights under the water, similar to the large flashing balls of light seen by Thor Heyerdahl and the crew of the *Kon-Tiki* below the surface of the Pacific Ocean. The most famous of all disappearance cases in the Bermuda triangle is that of the five Navy bombers that set out on a routine training flight from Fort Lauderdale, Florida, on December 5, 1945. After the mission was completed the five bombers headed back to Fort Lauderdale, but shortly before they were due to land they radioed that they were completely lost. They reported that their compasses were "going crazy" and their messages became more confused by the minute. Finally all radio contact was lost. A Martin Mariner rescue plane with a crew of thirteen was sent out to search for them. None of the five bombers, the search plane, or the crew members were ever seen or heard of again. The writer Lawrence Kusche contends that the mystery of the Bermuda Triangle is a manufactured one resulting from careless research by other writers. His arguments are fairly convincing. It may well be that the losses in the Bermuda Triangle are merely natural tragedies embellished and blown up into tales of legendary proportions. Yet it is odd that the United States Navy made its own film, *The Ocean Desert*, which reconstructed the frightening events of December 5, 1945, and showed a team of scientists exploring that part of the ocean and testing the Sargassum seaweed unique to the Bermudas. They were unable to find any connection between the odd, floating seaweed and the strange disappearances reputed to occur in that part of the ocean. As to the loss of its own aircraft, the Navy investigators had no explanation, and stated that they "were not able to make even a good guess as to what happened."

In the northeastern area of the Atlantic lies another stretch of sea, whose history of disappearances is even more bizarre than that of the Bermuda Triangle. At the thirty-fifth parallel, near the Azores, crews and passengers disappear but their vessels remain floating over the ocean like ghost ships. The most famous case to occur in this area was that of the *Marie Celeste*. In November, 1872, a British ship found the *Marie Celeste* sailing crewless. Inspection of the ship found everything to be in order.

There were no signs of any kind of disturbance. Breakfast was on the table waiting to be eaten. The only indication of anything unusual was the last entry in the captain's log: "A strange thing is happening to us . . ."

Odd disappearances are reported to occur at random on land. Whole armies have disappeared into thin air. During the Spanish War of Succession four thousand troops disappeared on a march through the Pyrenees. In 1858 six hundred fifty French Colonial troops marching toward Saigon vanished fifteen miles from the city. And more recently, in 1939, 2988 Chinese troops stationed south of Nanking vanished, leaving their camp in perfect order, their rifles neatly stacked. During World War II a Navy blimp patrolling the San Francisco Harbor was seen suddenly to soar up into a cloud only to reappear minus its two-man crew. In 1930 a Canadian Eskimo village was found completely deserted, yet half-cooked food sat over dead fires, precious possessions lay in their normal places, guns were propped up in doorways, and the bodies of starved dogs were tied to tree stumps. Ships, planes, riverboats, groups of people, individuals, and even small buildings—why do they vanish and where do they go?

In some cases the fate of those who "disappear" is partially explained by tiny heaps of ashes. Yet these are no ordinary cremations. The phenomenon of spontaneous combustion involves tremendous temperatures whose cause is quite unknown. One such case was that of Mary Reeser in St. Petersburg, Florida, in 1951. Only her shrunken skull, left foot, a few vertebrae, and the coil springs of her chair were found. It was calculated that she had burned up at a heat of 2500 degrees. Yet this intense heat had burned nothing else in the room. Its only visible effects were a crack in a mirror, some melted candles, and a film of soot on the walls starting four feet above the floor.

The human body itself is a house of mystery. Many of its functions remain secret. It lodges a phenomenal organ, the brain, whose full potential defies our comprehension. It weighs less than three pounds, yet this structure of over ten billion cells is infinitely more complex than the most sophisticated computer man is capable of building. But some researchers estimate that we use little more than 10 percent of our brain. What are the capabilities and purpose of the remaining portion?

For years there has been considerable skepticism regarding the powers of those who call themselves psychics. Despite this, many have used their unusual talents to earn a living by dousing for water, locating oil deposits for oil companies, diagnosing diseases for doctors, finding stolen property and bodies for police and other law enforcement agencies. Many such people, including Edgar Cayce, have developed their powers following accidents in which they sustained injuries to their heads or spinal cords. No one has yet resolved what the connection is between such injuries and the acquisition of unusual psychic powers, but it is apparent that we may all possess similar capabilities.

The meager inroads being made by researchers into the mysterious cerebral regions are already revolutionizing established concepts. Controlled scientific experiments have produced truly stunning results: Two subjects have experienced identical dreams through ESP while in hypnotic trances; time distortion has been achieved during hypnosis, enabling subjects to work out complicated designs, work plans, and mathematical problems in a matter of seconds, ideas that afterward can take hours to record: patients under postsurgical hypnosis have repeated the conversations of those around them while they were under general anesthesia; some individuals have the ability to hear light waves and see visual effects of sound waves; through biofeedback training subjects can learn to control brainwaves, perspiration, blood pressure, digestive juices, and heart rate.

Other animals, too, have strange powers. Particularly puzzling to man is the homing instinct of some animals, particularly birds. An astonishing case is that of the Manx shearwater, which was transported in a closed container to a place 3400 miles from its nest. The bird returned to its nest in twelve and a half days. Even more astounding is the cat who was left behind in New York when its master moved to California. Five months later the cat walked into its master's new home, jumped up onto its favorite armchair, and fell asleep. It had traveled at least 2300 miles.

In 1973 Peter Tompkins and Christopher Bird stunned the world with their bestselling book *The Secret Life of Plants*. In it they documented what had long been suspected—and more. Ordinary plants can feel emotions, diagnose diseases, act as lie detectors, read minds. This fascinating account of the physical, emotional, and spiritual relations between plants and man leaves the reader more perplexed than ever. How can plants possess such extraordinary powers?

The mysteries of life on Earth are countless. Those of outer space may be even more anomalous to the human mind. Every day strange things are happening, and some of these strange things come to our Earth from the celestial regions.

· 2 ·

RAINING FISH AND FROGS

Leonard Tillapaugh stared in amazement at the cloud of steam rising from the intruding object as it melted through the patch of snow and ice two and a half inches thick. He was a little dazed from his narrow escape. It had been a routine work day so far. He had spent the crisp, clear January morning spreading fertilizer on his fields. At about 11 o'clock he turned his tractor back toward the barn. As he passed under a large tree, something shot down from the sky, struck the tree, crashed down onto the tractor, narrowly missing Tillapaugh, and ricocheted onto a patch of ice a couple of feet away. He watched it melt through the ice and snow, then looked up at the sky. Visibility was excellent. Not a single aircraft was to be seen. Getting down from his tractor, Tillapaugh walked over and lifted the object from the pool of melted ice. About the size of a golf ball, it was covered with a black, brittle substance that broke off as he moved it in his fingers. Puzzled, he dropped it into his pocket and went on home.

Later in the day curious friends and neighbors were unable to identify Leonard Tillapaugh's find. The unanimous opinion was that it was a manufactured object, mainly because of its shape, which was rounded with one edge jagged as though broken off something.

Mysterious objects from the sky crashing into tractors are not everyday occurrences in the town of Carlisle, New York. Tillapaugh called the Schoharie County sheriff, Harvey Stoddard. The sheriff wasted little time in calling on him to look at the object and check out the tractor for broken parts. Finding no evidence to indicate that the object was part of the tractor, nor that it had been thrown up from the ground, Sheriff Stoddard decided to investigate the matter further. He was perplexed by the fact that the object had the appearance of a ceramiclike material, yet was extremely heavy for its size.

Unaware of the existence of the National Investigations Committee on Aerial Phenomena and other similar organizations, Sheriff Stoddard made every effort to identify the object using his local resources. He had it examined by two aircraft mechanics on the chance that it might have been a part from an airplane. The mechanics said that in their opinion it was not from any conventional aircraft used today. Nor were the New York State Police able to identify the object, but through prior contact with NICAP's regional investigator, Ernie Jahn, they knew where to turn for additional help.

By the time Ernie was reached on February 9, 1975, four weeks had passed since Leonard Tillapaugh's narrow escape from the hurtling object. Although it did not appear to be a meteorite or a piece of a satellite, Ernie's first move was to contact the Moonwatch Division of the Smithsonian Institution in Cambridge, Massachusetts. Utilizing their computer system, which is designed to give complete data on satellite and meteorite activity throughout the world, they reported that "nothing from anywhere in the world should have been in that particular area on January 12, 1975."

Ernie next turned to Northwestern University astronomer Dr. J. Allen Hynek, scientific consultant to the United States Air Force on UFO's and founder of the Center for UFO Studies, a core of twenty-six scientists concerned about the UFO issue. Dr. Hynek agreed to have initial testing carried out at Northwestern University. Without delay Sheriff Stoddard had the object shipped out to the laboratory, together with a brief report.

Meanwhile Ernie made a trip to Carlisle to meet with Sheriff Stoddard and visit the scene of the incident. Together the two men called on Leonard Tillapaugh and interviewed him at length. It was quite obvious that he was not fabricating the details of his experience. The sheriff later told Ernie that he was surprised that Tillapaugh, whom he and his deputies had known for years, had even bothered to take the time out from his farm to report the matter. A farmer with no scientific background, he was interested only in working his fields. To the busy farmer, time is money.

Sheriff Stoddard and Ernie re-examined the tractor.

Views of an unidentified object which fell from the sky

There was nothing missing from it. It was evident from its construction that the manifold was the only part from which a broken-off piece might be capable of generating so much heat. Any such damage would be immediately noticeable, and even after careful inspection they found no breakage. Even had the object been something the tractor kicked up out of the earth, it could not have been hot enough to melt right through the ice and snow. On the chance that another fragment of the object might be on the ground, they swept the area with a metal detector. Nothing was found.

When preliminary testing was completed at Northwestern University, the report revealed that analysis did not indicate that the object was a meteorite. It contained iron, had a rust coloration, and was magnetic. The researchers were unable to find similarities to any known terrestrial rocks and conjectured that it could have come from outer space. They also determined that the object had experienced extreme thermal shock.

A portion of the mysterious object then continued on its travels down to the Los Alamos Scientific Laboratory in New Mexico. There a team of researchers led by Dr. John Warren spent two months studying it. They, too, were perplexed by certain aspects of the case, but while their findings verified those of Northwestern University on the whole, there were some discrepancies in their analyses. One of the things that bothered them, but that they felt was of little significance, was the fact that there were a few basic elements missing that should have been present. However, it was possible that these elements had been deleted in prior testing. They, too, tended to eliminate the possibility of meteoric origin since the element nickel was absent. Because of the length of time it had taken for the object to reach their laboratory, they were unable to determine whether it had come from space. There were none of the usual marks that are present as a result of traveling through space, but such marks often disappear within a certain time period; also, the extensive testing and polishing could have removed them. Unlike the Northwestern investigators, they concluded that oxidation had probably occurred over a long period of time, not as a result of falling through Earth's atmosphere from outer space. The chemical composition was substantiated as being consistent with known compositions of common cast iron or so-called gray iron. Iron is a normal element of the earth, but the fact that it was cast meant that it had to be a manufactured substance. However, it was of such a poor grade that the cost of producing it would be greater than its value. Despite their ability to analyse it chemically the Los Alamos scientists were "unable to identify its functional origin or explain why Tillapaugh observed it to fall from the sky and melt ice."

While this incident was a first for the town of Carlisle, New York, it is not an unknown occurrence. On June 12, 1960, a sonic boom was heard in Quebec City, Canada. A fiery object fell out of the sky, splitting into two pieces, both of which fell into the St. Lawrence River. Analysis of the recovered chunks of hardware revealed that while there was nickel present, it was insufficient for the material to be of meteoric origin. It was considered to be of terrestrial origin, but further testing resulted in a number of unusual reactions not consistent with the normal behavior of terrestrial metal.

These are the rare cases where objects are scientifically analysed. The majority of falling objects remain untested and include such peculiar items as fish, frogs, stones, rocks, massive chunks of ice, pieces of flesh, toads, hail the size of golf balls, coal, worms, and shells. There are those who laughingly suggest that the lumps of ice fall from flying saucers as the occupants defrost their refrigerators! Silly as this idea is, it is no more peculiar than the very fact that all these odd items do fall out of the sky, sometimes in heavy showers.

They remain one of our unsolved mysteries, and Leonard Tillapaugh's object is no exception. After Dr. Warren carried out the final testing at the Los Alamos Scientific Laboratory, he could only tell Ernie, "It'll probably be an enigma such as the frogs that fall out of the sky. We know they're frogs. We know everything about them. We can analyse every part of them. But we can't tell you why they fall out of the sky, or where they come from."

· 3 ·

A DEADLY VISITOR
FROM SPACE

There was not the slightest hint of imminent disaster in that sparsely populated region of Siberia where the Tunguska River flows toward the great Yenisey River. It was June 30, 1908, nearly forty years before the United States exploded the first atomic bomb. The new day seemed like any other. Unsuspecting peasants were setting about their early morning chores while late risers remained lost in sleep. Far away in the Gobi Desert travelers stopped to watch a huge object passing through the dawn sky over China. It was not long before the first inhabitants of those lonely Siberian villages caught sight of the dazzling cylindrical body as it slid through their skies, leaving behind it a trail of multicolored smoke. With a deafening roar the object plunged toward the Siberian woods. Suddenly, with a searing, blinding flash of light, it exploded. As a fierce wave of heat shot across the countryside, boatmen hundreds of miles away were hurled into the river, horses tumbled to the ground, nomadic villages were annihilated, hundreds of reindeer vanished, and the ground heaved and shuddered, flinging helpless people into the air. Stunned and horrified, those who were not injured or unconscious watched uneasily as an eerie column of smoke rose up and up into the sky, finally billowing out at the top *in the shape of a mushroom.* Those closest to the center of the impact witnessed a horrendous change of scene. Where trees and grass and animals had existed only minutes before now lay a charred terrain clothed in a blanket of ashes. Directly below the point of the explosion charred trees remained upright. Extending beyond the center of impact to a forty-mile radius, trees were flattened with their tops pointing away from the epicenter. Seismographs all over the world were reacting, while barographs were recording the incredible air waves that were to encircle the entire world not once, but twice. It was perhaps the greatest instantaneous release of energy the world had ever known.

One of the strangest aftereffects occurred that night. It was witnessed not only in Siberia but throughout all Europe as well. There was no nightfall. Against a background of brilliant, colorful sunsets glowed massive silvery clouds tinged with a yellow-green light, which sometimes changed to a red or orange or rosy hue. At midnight people read their newspapers without the aid of artificial light. These conditions continued for a few nights but with lessening intensity. Since news of the cataclysmic explosion in the isolated Tunguska region had not reached the outer world, no one understood the origin of these extraordinary optical phenomena.

The Tungus, as the natives of that area of Siberia were known, were a superstitious people. Many of them believed this fiery visitor from the heavens to be Ogdy, the great god of fire. Fearful of his anger, none dared to venture near the fall site. Though stories of the disaster reached the newspapers of neighboring regions, little credence was given to them. The Tungus were well known for their hysteria and indeed, many of the details they related to local journalists were obviously born of their own fantasies. The story of this great explosion was almost lost as just another legend in the rich mythology of the Tungus. Fortunately, however, there were a few scientists in Russia whose attention was finally attracted by the rumors that leaked out to them over the next two decades. Because of the inaccessibility of the location and the dubious nature of the information, however, at first the Soviet scientific establishment was not eager to sponsor an expedition.

Thus almost twenty years passed before the first group of scientists penetrated the primeval Siberian forest to explore the still scorched site. After examining the scene and interviewing witnesses they determined that something from outer space had crashed down into that lonely area. They had left on the expedition expecting to find a meteorite. Though what they found did not concur with their knowledge of the then young science of meteoritics, they could find no other explanation. It went down on record as the Tunguska Meteorite. Repeated expeditions to the area during the prewar years failed to reveal evidence to support the meteoric theory. Never was a crater found, nor a single meteoric fragment.

Almost twenty more years passed before Dr. Alexander Kazantsev, Russian scientist and author, thought of an explanation for the baffling explosion. World War II had just ended. The United States had dropped the first atom bombs on Hiroshima and Nagasaki. Scores of scientists went to Japan to study the effects. As Dr. Kazantsev surveyed the devastated landscape where the city of Hiroshima had once stood, he had the uncanny feeling that he had seen this sight before. The tops of the trees had been snapped off directly beneath the center of the airborne explosion, while for miles around the trees were flattened with their tops pointing away from the epicenter. It seemed an almost familiar sight. Then it struck him. He had seen this phenomenon, known to be a characteristic only of nuclear explosions, in photographs of the site of the so-called Tunguska Meteorite.

The possibility of an atomic blast almost half a century before Hiroshima was so startling that the cautious scientist presented his theory in the form of science fiction in a popular magazine. The flattened trees of the Tunguska area, the mushroom cloud, and the subsequent light nights were all known characteristics of a nuclear explosion. But intrigued scientists knew that it would not be difficult to check for even more conclusive evidence. If the explosion had been nuclear, radioactive particles would still be detectable.

A new expedition set out for the Tunguska region. Their suspicions were confirmed. Tests on samples of trees, plants, ash, and soil revealed higher than normal quantities of radiation. Tiny particles of extraterrestrial matter were found lodged in the soil samples. These particles could not be identified as meteoric in origin, and they contained small amounts of metals, including copper and germanium, important in the construction of electrical and technical equipment. An unusually accelerated growth of trees and plants was evident in the area, yet another known after-effect of atomic explosions.

Further questioning of surviving witnesses uncovered other relevant details. A strange black rain had fallen in Central Siberia on June 30, 1908, just as it had in Hiroshima on August 6, 1945. During the weeks that followed, disgruntled herdsmen had watched their reindeer succumb to an unknown disease, which produced scabs on their bodies similar to the radiation blisters found on cattle in New Mexico after their exposure to the radiation debris of the experimental atom bomb at Alamagordo. Based on the witnesses' reports as well as on ballistic wave evidence, a careful reconstruction of the flight path showed that at the last stage of its journey the visitor from space had changed its course over the Tunguska forest from an eastward to a westward direction.

The general consensus of the scientific study team was that on June 30, 1908, some sort of atomic-powered apparatus weighing over fifty thousand tons exploded over the Siberian forest at an altitude of just over three miles. Dr. Kazantsev believes that apparatus to have been an extraterrestrial craft that was in the process of landing when its atomic engines exploded.

Some scientists today believe that the 1908 explosion can still be explained in terms of meteor or comet impact despite the contrary evidence. Dr. Felix Zigel of the Moscow Aviation Institute, a leading proponent of UFO's, defies these suggestions and states that not only is it unfeasible for a comet to change its course in mid-air but that also, had the visitor been a comet, it would have been noticed by astronomers long before it impacted Earth. He concludes that it must be classified as a UFO.

One body of scientific opinion proposes an intriguing antimatter theory. They hypothesize that a small quantity of antimatter may have leaked, without changing, through the barriers between dimensions and collided with the positive atoms of our own world.

Whether the answer to the mystery lies in one of these explanations or in one as yet not contemplated, there is obviously little agreement on the matter. Yet this mighty explosion, hundreds of times more powerful than that at Hiroshima, did occur. That much is without doubt. The identity of that cylindrical object that sailed through our skies in 1908, however, will probably remain a mystery to mankind.

Above: The site of the 1908 explosion in Siberia
Below: Hiroshima in 1945 after the atom bomb was dropped
(*From the motion picture* The Force Beyond)

· 4 ·

WHAT ARE TEKTITES?

Examining the glassy object he held in his hand, he knew there was something strange about it. Its odd shape and peculiar markings distinguished it from the other rocks scattered on the ground. The young Charles Darwin had reached Australia toward the end of a world-wide voyage of exploration that had begun in 1831 and would not return him to his home shores until 1836. Years later his world-shaking theory on the origin of species overshadowed his distinction of being the first person to discover an australite. Australites, and similar objects found in other parts of the world, are known today under the collective name "tektite," derived from the Greek word "tektos," meaning "molten."

Tektites are on display in many museums of natural history, where curious visitors hazard fanciful suggestions as to what these bizarre objects might be. Geologists and geophysicists have been studying them for years, and while they are able to define their age, composition, and the processes that have influenced their structural formation, it is their origin that remains unsolved.

Tektites are small glassy objects, ranging in size from that of a pinhead to that of a man's head and in weight from fractions of an ounce to nearly a pound. Some of their shapes resemble splash forms such as teardrops, spheroids, buttons, cylinders, dumbbells, disks, and rods, while others display totally irregular shapes. In reflected light tektites appear dark, but thin edges and sections transmit light and reveal colors ranging from yellow to bottle green and from olive brown to dark brown to black.

They are composed largely of silica (up to 80 percent),

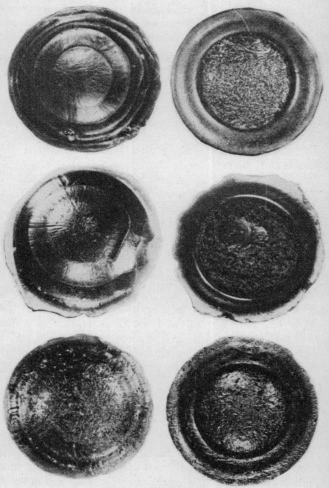

Button-shaped tektites
(Courtesy John A. O'Keefe and George Baker)

which gives them their characteristic glassy appearance. They also contain small quantities of oxides such as aluminum, iron, magnesium, calcium, sodium, and potassium. They bear no geological or mineralogical affinity to any rock chemistry on Earth. The oldest tektites found are about forty-five million years old, the youngest only a few thousand.

Tektites are found in specific areas of the world, widely strewn in large groups as if some giant hand had reached down out of the sky and sprinkled them over the land.

They are usually named after the region where they are found. In most cases the connection is obvious, but where it is not the name may be derived from a geologic formation or from some other distinctive feature of the region. Remarkably, many independently discovered strewn fields in various parts of the world have turned out to be part of the same group. Thus we have the North American group, consisting of bediasites (named after the Indian tribe) from Texas, the georgiaites from Georgia, and a single specimen found at Martha's Vineyard in Massachusetts; the Czechoslovakian group, consisting of moldavites (after the Moldav River) from Moravia and Bohemia; a small group of Ivory Coast tektites in Africa; and the Australasia group, the most abundant and widely spread of the known groups, which consists of several million specimens. This last group includes the Philippines (philippinites or rizalites), Australia (australites), Indonesia (javaites from Borneo and billitonites from the Isle of Billiton in the Java Sea), and Southeast Asia (indochinites).

Microtektites have been found in ocean sediments. These tiny forms of glass are of the same age and composition as nearby corresponding land tektites with essentially the same splash-form shapes but range from pinhead size down to about a twenty-fifth of a millimeter. Such a group are the microtektites found in the Atlantic just off the Ivory Coast, where a small number of tektites have been found. The tiny glass particles discovered in the South Pacific, dating back seven hundred thousand years and related to the Australia mainland tektites, were deposited at about the same time as the reversal of Earth's magnetic field. There are those who consider the intriguing possibility that a large meteorite impact could have caused both the reversal and the tektites.

Among early theories of their origin was the belief that tektites could be the fragments of a lost, shattered planet of the solar system. Some advocated the theory that they were the consequence of lightning striking Earth. However, while lightning is known to fuse sand occasionally, the shapes that result do not match those of tektites. Others proposed that they were produced by volcanic action but, again, while it is true that glass is produced in volcanoes, it does not match the chemical composition of tektites. Moreover, volcanoes are not features common to the areas where tektites have been found. Some suggested that a volcanic eruption or similar upheaval on the moon hurled thousands of these tiny objects out into space, where they went into an Earth orbit and eventually fell to the ground.

It is generally agreed today that tektites are the result of an impact somewhere on Earth or on the moon since many specimens contain tiny nickel-iron spherules of definite meteoric origin. However, there is still much debate as to which of these celestial bodies is the true source. Planets far from Earth or the moon are considered improbable because evidence of long exposure to cosmic rays in space is absent in tektites.

One school of thought contends that tektites are stones thrown up by the impact of meteorites, asteroids, or the heads of comets as they crashed into Earth. In this case craters would still be evident, for the tektites are not old enough to allow time for the complete erosion and disappearance of such impact areas. In only two cases are there craters present that could give some support to this theory. The Ivory Coast tektites appear to be approximately the same age as the Bosumtwi Crater in neighboring Ghana, and the Czechoslovakian tektites are approximately the same age as the not too distant Ries Kessel Crater in southern Germany. Yet no rocks bearing any similarity to tektite compositon have been found at either of these craters. In other cases no crater of the proper age is present at all, and suggestions that the impact could have occurred in the open sea are rejected because there would still be telltale signs of the huge tidal wave that would have ensued.

Other believers in the terrestrial impact theory point out that the crater might be far removed from the tektites. The collision could have been of such tremendous force that it melted terrestrial rock and hurled it way out into an Earth orbit. As the orbit decayed, the tektites would have fallen to Earth, the long passages through the atmosphere producing the heat that melted the rock fragments, causing them to assume the odd shapes peculiar to tektites.

It can be deduced from the constitution of tektites that they did originate at an extremely high temperature and after solidifying were subjected to further surface melting. Experiments have demonstrated that the unique forms and curious surface sculpture can be reproduced by a two-step process. First, the surfaces of tektite glass are aerodynamically melted and eroded at hypervelocities corresponding to entry into Earth's atmosphere from space. This is followed by slight chemical decomposition to simulate natural decomposition as a result of exposure to geologic and weathering processes. In particular, the aerodynamic evidence for the Australasian tektites indicates that their velocity of atmosphere entry corresponds to that of trajectories originating from the moon. In fact, the geographic distribution pattern of Australasian tektites can be identified with the particular pattern that would result from the ejection of material from one of the prominent rays of the lunar crater Tycho.

John O'Keefe, Assistant Chief of the Theoretical Division of NASA's Goddard Space Flight Center, supports the ever more popular theory that tektites originated on the lunar surface. Experiments have shown that some of the debris from any high speed impact will achieve a velocity greater than that of the impacting object. Thus when meteorites crash into the moon, traveling at the same speeds they possessed in space because there is no atmosphere to slow them down, lunar material will be blasted out into space. Most of this material goes into orbit around the sun, while a small fraction falls directly to Earth and a larger portion is trapped in orbit around Earth. During millions of years Earth probably sweeps up large amounts of the sun-circling debris, of which tektites could make up only a tiny portion. O'Keefe believes that Earth is strewn with millions of tons of rock and dust from the surface of the moon but that they go unnoticed because they do not bear the distinctive marks and forms of tektites. Indeed, he feels it is very likely that most people have at one time or another set eyes on them.

O'Keefe proposes that a large chunk of lunar debris traveling in an elliptical orbit around Earth might decay almost to a sphere as a result of slowing down during repeated passages through Earth's atmosphere. Gravitational and other stresses would cause it to break into smaller fragments. These fragments, the parent bodies of tektites, would each have a different orbit and therefore a different speed. The extreme heating processes would form a molten layer thick enough to shed drops that would solidify into tektites. As they fell to Earth they would be sculptured by the air stream. The fragment traveling fastest with the shortest orbit would be the first to scatter tektites across the land surface and would be followed at successive intervals by the remaining slower fragments with longer orbits. This would explain why there are often independently strewn fields within one group of tektites, and the width of the Australasian field, for example, would be accounted for by the distance Earth had turned on its axis between each successive orbit.

Further evidence to support this theory is the fact that during John Glenn's 1962 MA-6 flight, the sustainer rocket, which had been put into an orbit much like that of the capsule, came apart after a number of orbits. The widely scattered pieces were picked up at various points in South Africa along a strip more than five hundred miles long and over sixty miles wide.

It was hoped that analysis of samples brought from the moon by Apollos 11 and 12 would answer the question once and for all, but for the most part, the chemical structures do not match. However, microtektites have revealed compositions similar to those of lunar rocks, and some lunar rocks have proved to bear impressive similarities to tektites in their percent distribution of components.

Another dashing blow to the otherwise rather convincing theory of lunar origin is the presence of gases in the tiny sealed cavities of some tektites. Analysis of these gases reveals oxygen, nitrogen, and argon in the same proportions as in Earth's atmosphere. Since there are no apparent leaks, the gases would have to have been trapped during the tektites' liquid state, thus indicating a terrestrial origin.

The controversy continues. Perhaps they really are pieces of the moon, but when it comes right down to proving positively where tektites come from and what they are, the problem remains in the realm of speculation.

· 5 ·

THE MYSTERY OF
THE CELESTIAL PARADE

"Some dire calamity is coming to the Earth!" cried one hysterical lady, almost fainting in terror.

The crowds in the streets stared upward.

"No," replied another, "they must be souls going to heaven."

"Only beauty, beauty!" said a more lucid witness of the incredible luminous procession that filed across the Sunday evening sky.

They glided along so leisurely and did not seem to be falling as meteors usually do, but kept a straight course, about forty-five degrees, or a little more, above the horizon. Our first impression was that a fleet of illuminated airships of monstrous size were passing. The incandescent fragments themselves formed what to us looked like the illuminations, while the tails seemed to make the frame of the machine. Sometimes there would be just a single collection, forming a single ship; then in a half-minute several collections would pass, looking like ships traveling in company.

It was February 9, 1913. That night hundreds of people from Central Canada right across the United States to Bermuda and beyond witnessed a most astounding phenomenon. At about 9:05 p.m. there suddenly appeared in the northwestern sky a fiery red body, which grew larger and larger as it came closer. A long tail became visible behind it. Some observers stated that it was a single object, some that it was made up of two distinct parts, and others that there were three parts, all traveling together and each followed by a long tail.

The front of the object was somewhat brighter than the rest but the overall color was a fiery red or golden yellow. The tail seemed to some like the glare from the open door of a fiercely burning furnace, while to others it looked like the illumination from a search light and to others like a stream of sparks blowing from a burning chimney in a strong wind.

The first impression of many observers was that someone had set off a great skyrocket. Indeed, the streaming tail behind it and the color of both the head and tail resembled a rocket. But this "rocket" showed no signs of falling earthward. Instead it flew forward on a perfectly horizontal path with a peculiar, majestic deliberation. Without the least apparent drop in altitude it continued on its course to the southwest, disappearing into the distance.

It is a well-known fact that meteors, or shooting stars, remain visible for only a few seconds and that the brilliant ones fall to Earth very rapidly, as one commentator on the event remarked, "in a mighty hurry to reach their destination." But here were objects moving along at a stately, leisurely pace giving those below the time to make as many wishes as they desired. Some reported that just before this object disappeared, it burst, leaving behind it a trail of stars.

The startled observers scarcely had the time to catch their bated breath when more lights emerged from the same spot in the northwestern sky, proceeding along the same course. Their tails streaming behind them, slightly shorter and dimmer than the first object, they traveled at the same slow, deliberate pace in twos or threes or fours.

Gradually the objects diminished in size, until the last ones were mere red sparks, some being snuffed out before reaching the point in the southeastern sky where the others had disappeared from view. Several reports stated that

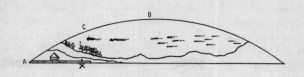

B
C
A
X

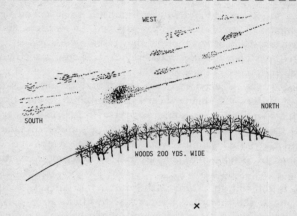

WEST

NORTH

SOUTH

WOODS 200 YDS. WIDE

×

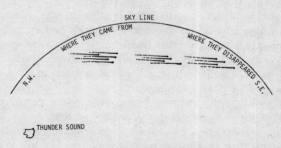

SKY LINE

WHERE THEY CAME FROM

WHERE THEY DISAPPEARED S.E.

N.W.

THUNDER SOUND

×MY POSITION

The mysterious celestial parade:
sketches by witnesses in three different locations.
In each drawing, *X* marks the position of the observer.

near the middle of the great procession was a large bright red star without a tail and that a similar star brought up the rear.

Most of the witnesses were impressed by the slow, majestic movement of the objects and by the perfect formation they maintained. In trying to describe what they had seen, some compared them to a fleet of airships, with lights on either side and forward and aft, some called up the image of great battleships attended by cruisers and destroyers, while others thought they resembled a brilliantly lighted passenger train, traveling in broken-up sections and seen from a distance.

Just as the objects were vanishing, and in some cases shortly afterward, many heard a rumbling sound like distant thunder, or, as some observers stated, like a carriage passing over rough roads or over a bridge. In some places three such sounds were heard successively and a number of people felt the ground shuddering beneath them.

It is difficult to estimate the number of objects seen that night; the majority of reports state fifteen to twenty, but some claim sixty to a hundred, while others said that there were thousands. Such discrepancies could be attributed to the differing visual ability of witnesses, some of whom were able to distinguish many parts and fragments where others saw only one body. The only person known to have viewed the spectacle with any instrumental assistance was Cecil Carley, a high school student in Trenton, Ontario. "There were about ten groups in all," he reported, "and each group, as seen through the opera glass, consisted of from twenty to forty smaller meteors."

It is mainly due to the bold efforts of Professor C. A. Chant of Toronto University, editor of the *Journal of the Royal Astronomical Society of Canada*, that we have as much information on the extraordinary nighttime procession as we do. Following requests obligingly published by daily newspapers across the country, he received hundreds of letters from eyewitnesses. The accounts varied in detail, but after a painstaking study Chant was able to put together most of the pieces of the puzzle. Despite this, the picture still was not clear, for the facts did not concur with any known meteoric event. Using only observations on which he, as a scientist, felt he had particular reason to depend, he made his calculations.

The average duration of the procession's visibility to the gazing viewers below was a little over three minutes. The height of the objects above the ground was calculated to be 26 miles, and their speed somewhere between 5 and 10 miles per second, far too low and far too slow for a meteor. Chant's reports came in from people on a track spanning northwest to southeast from Mortlach, Saskatchewan, to a point northeast of Bermuda, a distance of twenty-five hundred miles, one-tenth of Earth's circumference. The greatest distance any meteor has ever been known to travel is fifteen hundred miles.

The numerous reports also revealed the fact that during a few hours before and after the great display several other striking "meteors" were observed. Particularly odd were observations of a similar procession on the same trajectory as the first, but seen five hours later at about 2:30 a.m. Scientists of the day were particularly confused by this repetition of the phenomenon over the *same* route after Earth had turned through a 75-degree angle.

But the mystery thickened when the following afternoon, February 10, at 2 o'clock in the afternoon, the occupants of a tall building in Toronto saw dark objects moving out over the lake from west to east in three groups and then returning west in more scattered formation, about seven or eight in all. They were not seen clearly enough to determine their nature, but they did not seem to be clouds or birds or smoke and it was suggested at the time that perhaps they were airships cruising over the city.

Chant's prompt investigations were followed up over the next three years by W. F. Denning of England. Denning opened his first report with the remark that he had been watching the heavens since 1865 and had never seen anything like it. "The wonderful stream of successive meteors," he said, "seems, like Saturn's rings, without a parallel." Despite this, he made a disputation of Chant's calculations that seemed to be based more on what should have been than on what was. Denning discovered two more marine sightings, however, which extended the observed path of the procession as far as Cape São Roque, at the northeasternmost corner of Brazil, a total distance of more than six thousand miles. Nothing in the annals of meteoritics can compare with this path length.

There were varying opinions among the handful of scientists who took the time to look into the great aerial procession. Chant concluded that the group of objects had been traveling through space, probably in an orbit around the sun, and that on coming near Earth they were captured by it. As temporary satellites of Earth, maintaining a circular orbit practically parallel to Earth's surface, they were slowly consumed by atmospheric friction.

Scientists Davidson, Hoffmeister, and Fisher (quoted by Alexander D. Mebane in *Meteoritic Magazine,* Vol. 4, 1956), were disturbed by the seeming impossibility of such an orbit. Since Earth is not a perfect sphere but is slightly flattened at the poles, bulging at the equator, they contend that an object traveling only 26 miles above the ground in Ontario would collide with the equatorial bulge before reaching the equator; the air resistance in any case should prohibit a flight that long except by bodies of an enormous size. Disregarding Chant's height determination of 26 miles, they hypothesized a vertically extended stack of large meteorites, whose lower end reached down to the 30- or 40-mile level. Thus the stack was the actual satellite while the processions witnessed along its path

Map showing path of the 1913 event:
A marks Mortlach, Saskatchewan, where it was first seen.
B marks the point where it passed Bermuda.
C marks the location at which it was last seen,
just off Cape São Roque, Brazil.

were the successive peeling off of its lower part by air friction as the stack slowly lost altitude on its orbital flight. This assumption would account for the similarity of the display at all points of observation without requiring any single meteorite to traverse more than a fraction of the whole trajectory.

Yet discrepancies in the various descriptions led scientist Alexander D. Mebane, a one-time contributor to early NICAP studies, to suspect that Chant erred in fitting all of the observations to a single line. He feels that perhaps there were several groups of fireballs seen in different areas of Canada and the United States.

C. C. Wylie had presented an analysis of the Toronto observations intended to show that they could be interpreted as a meteor shower localized over that area, unconnected with the distant observations. Mebane commented that "Wylie's views, presumably because they were regarded as the most 'conservative,' have been accepted by some, although they are not likely to seem plausible to those who have examined the extensive observational data."

NASA's John O'Keefe, who believes that the objects were almost certainly a group of small Earth satellites moving in an orbit of low eccentricity, perhaps originating on the moon, has considered the possibility of there being a connection between the 1913 phenomenon and tektites, particularly since ablation studies of tektites have indicated similar velocities.

Researcher and author Charles Fort adopted the approach that there was no connection between the various observations and that each was a local phenomenon whose linkage with the others is only a product of the imagination. He suggested that while displays elsewhere may have been ordinary meteors, that seen in Toronto was a fleet of extraterrestrial spacecraft.

Researchers have never reached a satisfactory conclusion.

The event was classified under the name "Cyrillids," named for the feast day of St. Cyril of Alexandria on which it occurred. Though often referred to as a meteor shower, one thing is certain: its characteristics contradict all established patterns of meteor showers. Already mentioned are the low height, low speed, horizontal trajectory, duration of visibility, and prolonged course. Also to be considered is that while meteor showers occur frequently throughout the year, they arrive so rarely in February that there are actually ten days in that month when none occur. Moreover, not a single fragment has ever been found.

What was it that paraded across our skies that night? Where did it come from? Where did it go?

· 6 ·

POSSIBLE IMPOSSIBILITIES!

Many people feel that visitation by extraterrestrial spacecraft is impossible!

But then frogs falling from the sky is impossible! The disappearance of an entire army into thin air is impossible! The spontaneous combustion of human bodies is impossible! Psychic prediction is impossible! A meteor shower that remains visible for a distance of over six thousand miles is impossible! So continues the list of seemingly possible impossibilities.

Speculation regarding extraterrestrial visitation is often haughtily put down as being almost totally impossible because "according to the laws of physics matter cannot travel faster than the speed of light," making interstellar travel impractical and unlikely. Such skeptics may in fact be speaking the truth. But as the British philosopher of science, Sir Karl Popper, said, "Every scientific statement must remain tentative for ever." We cannot deny the evidence of thousands of UFO witnesses purely on the grounds that what they have seen is impossible. Remembering that UFO does not mean "flying saucer," there is no proof that UFO's, whatever they may be, are not phenomena of earthly origin. But the possibility exists that UFO's are extraterrestrial craft visiting Earth from outer space.

PART

Two

EXTRATERRESTRIAL
LIFE

WHAT IS OUT
IN SPACE?

The flames began to flicker around his feet and ankles. The former monk obstinately refused to accept the cross being held out to him. On that February day in 1600 Giordano Bruno was burned to death at the stake in Rome's Campo de' Fiori for adhering to beliefs in opposition to accepted church doctrine of the time. Today many of those theories are known facts. Not only did Bruno support the heretical Copernican theory that, instead of the sun circling Earth, Earth circles the sun, but he had the audacity to propose that we are not alone in the universe, that there are other planets out in space inhabited by intelligent creatures.

In 1835 it was no longer dangerous to make such assertions. Richard Locke, an English journalist living in the United States, ran a series of articles in the New York *Sun* on extraordinary astronomical discoveries being made with the use of a "new" type of telescope. The high point of the startling revelations was the description of lunar bat men, four-foot-high, winged creatures whose faces were a mixture of orangutan and human being. Since Sir John Herschel, the astronomer who was supposedly making these observations, was in South Africa at the time, slow communications prevented any immediate denial of these fallacious reports. It was several weeks before the hoax was exposed, but during that time hundreds of people had wholeheartedly accepted the story, and a group of ladies in Massachusetts had begun plans to convert the bat men to Christianity.

Today most scientists agree that intelligent life probably does exist elsewhere in the universe, though not on other planets within our own solar system. Before considering the prospect of aliens visiting our Earth, we must look into the problem of which planets might be inhabited and how many there are.

First, one must understand the basic composition of the universe. Our Earth is one of nine nonluminous bodies or planets that orbit a huge sphere of hot gas known as the sun. Although we are not aware of the movement, Earth is in fact being whirled through space at the tremendous rate of 18.5 miles per second on its year-long journey around the sun. The closest planet to the sun is Mercury, then Venus, then Earth, then Mars. Beyond Mars is a belt of miniature planets known as the asteroids. Then come the giant planets, Jupiter, Saturn, Uranus, and Neptune. Another small planet, Pluto, is the ninth planet on the perimeter of the system. Among them the planets have thirty-two natural satellites called moons, of which

Earth has one. The smallest bodies orbiting the sun are comets and meteors. A comet, in fact, is merely a conglomeration of tiny particles surrounded by a haze of thin gas, sometimes with a long tail. Meteors are tiny bodies, usually no larger than grains of sand, which often make themselves visible to human beings when they enter Earth's atmosphere and burn up as "shooting stars." Larger bodies known as meteorites survive the fall to the ground where they sometimes explode, scattering fragments and leaving large craters. Together with dust and gas, all these bodies—the sun, the planets, the moons, the asteroids, comets, and meteors—make up what is called a solar system.

Every star that we see in the night sky is another sun like ours. In fact, our sun is only one among one hundred billion stars that form a star system or galaxy. Although in popular usage the name Milky Way is often used to refer to a concentration of stars at the center of the system that stretch across the sky on clear moonless nights like a white pathway, it is in fact the name of the whole galaxy of which we are a part. In a flattened spiral structure shaped like two fried eggs back to back, the stars of the galaxy revolve around the center. The Milky Way system measures about 600 light years in thickness and 100,000 light years across, our solar system being about two-thirds out from the center. Light year measurements are used because distances in space are so vast that normal mileage becomes clumsy. A light year is the distance a ray of light or radio signal travels in one year; roughly six trillion miles. Our sun's nearest neighbor, a star named Alpha Centauri, is 4.3 light years away and, in fact, when we look at that star we are, in effect, looking into the past for we are seeing the light that it projected 4.3 years ago.

About one hundred billion galaxies make up the known universe. Not all of them have our system's wheel-shaped spiral formation. Some are round, some are elliptical, and some are irregular. The nearest galaxies are the Large and Small Magellanic Clouds, two satellites of our galaxy that contain a few billion stars each. Our next nearest galactic neighbor, the Andromeda Galaxy, resembles ours in size, shape, and number of stars and is a mere 2,000,000 light years away! Most galaxies occur in clusters, each cluster containing from three to ten thousand galaxies. The Milky Way system and the Andromeda Galaxy belong to a small cluster called the Local Group, which includes about a dozen other galaxies. These clusters form the largest systems of organized matter known to human beings to date.

The colossal distances that stretch across and between the galaxies are hard for the human mind to comprehend. But the situation is even more fantastic when we consider the fact that the whole universe is in a constant state of expansion. This means that the galaxies are racing away from one another at very high speeds, some of them at well over 100,000 miles per second.

Before going on to conjecture where in this vast universe life might exist, we should take note of the basic requirements for the presence of life as we know it. Unfortunately, no one was around on this planet to witness and record the origin of life. Scientists have had to figure out the answer through considerable analysis and experimentation. It is believed that the first living organisms were created in the oceans where simple molecules, produced by lightning and ultraviolet rays, drifted about, occasionally colliding with other molecules at just the right angle to join together to form new and larger molecules. A series of such collisions could have resulted in the eventual construction of the complicated molecules of the cell: DNA, RNA, and proteins. The essential medium in this process is an abundant water supply that allows the molecules to move about and collide. Other fluid mediums such as liquid ammonia might qualify, but, in the case of ammonia, the temperature would have to be extremely low since it

does not convert from vapor to liquid until cooled to about
−26 degrees Fahrenheit. The early steps of the process
have been successfully duplicated under laboratory conditions, though nothing that could be called living has yet
been achieved. One of the problems is the considerable
time lapse necessary. It took a few billion years for intelligent life to develop on Earth.

Within our own solar system there is little likelihood
of intelligent life having evolved except on Earth. However, the search for simpler life forms continues with some
optimism. Early exploration is not always conclusive. We
must compare our early visits to other planets with those
of a hypothetical alien who might land on Earth. If he,
or she, or it, were to land in the middle of the Sahara
Desert, this planet might be judged a very sterile way-
station in space. Photographic evidence can be even more
misleading. Early satellite photographs of our own Earth
gave the impression that some of our most heavily populated and densely vegetated regions were deserted and
barren.

In his first visits to the moon man may have missed
some potential discoveries, but it is certain that life is not
one of them. The structural elements of the moon and its
lack of water and atmosphere make it a totally hostile environment for the support of any kind of life form.

The great distances between the sun and the planets
beyond the asteroids make them unlikely candidates for
life-supporting habitats. Pluto is so distant that we know
little about it except that it is similar to Earth in size and
composition and must be far too cold to support any form
of life. The four giant planets, Neptune, Uranus, Saturn,
and Jupiter, are of exceedingly low density, being made
up mainly of the lightest elements, hydrogen and helium.
Saturn, in fact, is even less dense than water. Jupiter, the
largest planet in the solar system, is so massive that its
correspondingly mighty force of gravity keeps a tenacious

hold on all the gases of its original atmosphere, including ammonia, methane, and water, the common compounds of hydrogen. These components are believed to have played an essential part in the initial development of life on Earth. The possibility arises that simple life forms may have developed on Jupiter. Dr. Robert Jastrow, founder and director of the Goddard Institute for Space Studies, postulates that the −300 degrees Fahrenheit temperature of Jupiter's cloud level is not as disenchanting as it might seem when we consider that Earth's temperature above the clouds at 30,000 feet is usually −60 degrees Fahrenheit. Whether Jupiter has an actual surface or just an atmosphere that increases in density until it reaches a liquid state, it is quite probable that a layer exists where the temperature is suitable for the creation and sustainment of life. It would not be the kind of oxygen-breathing life that we know, but perhaps it will not be too many years before a spacecraft from Earth will be able to give us a more complete picture.

Of the three other planets between the asteroid belt and the sun, Mercury would seem inordinately unhospitable because of its proximity to the sun. Its desolate, rocky surface is alternately baked on the side facing the sun and frozen on the side facing away. Between Mercury and Earth lies the planet Venus, once believed by some to be a tropical paradise. Russian and American spacecraft have revealed it to be a sizzling inferno. Twenty-three million miles closer to the sun than Earth, it receives twice the intensity of sunlight. Dr. Jastrow believes that its incredible surface temperature of over 900 degrees Fahrenheit is the result of heat being trapped by the dense atmosphere of carbon dioxide. Water, in the form of vapor, is extremely sparse. And completing the hellish picture is the probability that the thick clouds on Venus are made up of tiny drops of sulfuric acid.

Mars gives us cause for hope. One and a half times

further from the sun than Earth is, Mars's climate is cold but not unbearable. Antaractic winter temperatures sometimes rise to as much as 70 degrees along the equator during the summer. Although moisture in the atmosphere is not sufficient for the initial formation of living organisms, it could suffice for the sustainment of simple life forms, forms that might have developed under different conditions and adapted to a drier climate. It was hoped that Russian and American probes might prove that Mars did once have enough water in liquid form for life to have begun its long, slow process of development. The missions of the 1960s proved disappointing. Pictures of a 10-degree area divulged a Martian landscape similar to the lunar surface, pocked with craters and without the slightest indication of water erosion. Hope began to dissipate. It began to seem that the living organism might be a fluke peculiar to the planet Earth. But the desire to find companions in space, even of the simplest kind, prevailed. The search continued, and 1972 brought auspicious surprises. Mariner 9, orbiting Mars, was able to map the entire surface of the planet and transmit pictures of remarkable quality back to Earth. Photographs of areas never seen before were analyzed and produced startling conclusions. Volcanoes, canyons, and other signs of geologic activity and water erosion made up a landscape similar to that of our planet. One of the volcanoes, *Nix Olympica*, is twice as large as any earthly volcano. Dr. Jastrow points out that all Earth's water is believed to have come out of the interior of the planet in the form of steam escaping from molten rock as it gushed out of erupting volcanoes. Thus the discovery of great mounds of congealed lava on Mars indicates that water was at some stage brought up to the surface by molten rock. Meandering riverbeds and a system of braided channels are identical to those formed by silt-laden rivers on Earth. Photographs of the Martian canyon *Valles Marineris* disclose an astonishing similarity to the Grand Canyon. But there is a difference: The *Valles Marineris* is fourteen times as long and as much as four times as wide as the Grand Canyon. The deep tributaries of the Grand Canyon were formed by water erosion over a period of millions of years. The consensus of the scientific world was that at one time in its history Mars had an abundant supply of water on its surface. Because of this conclusion Mariner 9 brought great hope that hardy survivors of such equitable conditions might still exist today.

A new mission was planned. In 1975 Viking I and Viking II were launched. As they approached the red planet and began to orbit in search of suitable landing sites, the pictures they transmitted back to Earth showed in even greater detail the irrefutable evidence of extensive water erosion across the planet's surface. The gigantic volcanoes photographed made those on Earth seem dwarflike. *Olympus Mons*, a Martian volcano measuring almost four hundred miles across the base and looming to an incredible height of just over fifteen miles, may well be, say NASA scientists, the largest volcano in the entire solar system.

In 1976 the two Viking spacecraft made their historic soft landings on Mars. The first color photographs to be sent back to Earth showed the rust-colored Martian landscape, rocky and desolate, stretched out beneath a pink sky. One of the Viking's main objectives was the search for life. It was understood, however, that the failure to discover life processes might merely be an indication of having chosen the wrong landing site or of having made incorrect assumptions about the nature of the life processes. NASA scientists knew that whatever life might exist there would almost certainly be microbial.

Since it was obvious that no living organism could survive the intensive bombardment of ultraviolet radiation on the surface, the explorers took soil samples from under

A gigantic valley with branching tributaries on the surface
of Mars, photographed by Mariner 9 *(Courtesy NASA)*

small rocks. Portions of these samples were distributed to separate chambers to be subjected to three different biology experiments. One test was based on the premise of life being sustained through a process known as photosynthesis. On Earth photosynthesis occurs when green plants, using the sun as a source of energy, consume carbon dioxide and, by combining it with water and salts, form the organic compounds of which they are made. In the Viking experiment carbon dioxide that had been labeled with a radioactive tracer was substituted for part of the natural atmospheric gas in the test chamber and the chamber illuminated by artificial sunlight. After a few days the remaining gas was expelled from the chamber and the soil sample heated to liberate any of the radioactively labeled carbon dioxide that it might have assimilated in a photosynthetic process. This liberated gas was then measured.

The second experiment was based on the premise of life being sustained by nourishment from organic materials, rather than through photosynthesis. This time the sample was "fed" with organic compounds containing labeled radioactive carbon. Organisms consuming such nourishment could excrete the carbon as radioactive gas, which can then be measured.

The third experiment was based on the premise of respiration, or the exchange of chemicals between organisms and the atmosphere. In this case the soil sample was moistened with nutrients and the atmosphere of the chamber monitored for changes in the composition of the gases.

The surprisingly complicated results of these tests, sometimes positive, sometimes contradictory, have left NASA scientists confused. The expectation that the Viking mission would resolve the age-old controversy over the existence or nonexistence of life on Mars remains unfulfilled. It is uncertain if the results of the tests should be ascribed to genuine biological activity within the Martian soil, to unusual chemical properties of the soil, or to a slight inaccuracy in the testing equipment. In the photosynthetic test the quantity of labeled gas measured suggested that photosynthesis might have taken place, yet control tests, in which the sample was heated prior to testing in order to kill off anything that might be living, also indicated a positive though much weaker reaction. In the second test the release of radioactive carbon dioxide was unexpectedly high, but scientists realized that certain peroxides believed to exist in the soil could have caused this to occur, thus making it a chemical rather than a biological reaction. The same explanation might also be applicable to the gas exchange experiment in which oxygen was released by the sample into the atmosphere at an unexpectedly high rate. No scientist wants the embarrassment of coming to the wrong conclusion on such an important issue as this. Cautious officials at NASA declared the Viking findings to be inconclusive.

Dr. Jastrow, however, believes that the key to the problem lies in the comparison between the separate results elicited at the two different landing sites. The strongest clue, he feels, comes from the gas exchange test. The soil at the site of Viking II was much damper and contained less oxygen than that at the Viking I site. If oxygen was released as a chemical reaction to moisture combining with the soil's peroxide content, then the Viking II sample should have released less oxygen than the Viking I sample. Yet this was not the case. The release of oxygen from the Viking II sample was much greater than that from the Viking I sample. Dr. Jastrow believes that this negates the possibility of it being a chemical reaction. "It is not one hundred percent assurance," he says, "but the evidence indicates that there is life, or what we call life, on the planet Mars."

Looking at our place in the universe as a whole, Dr. J.

Allen Hynek has conjured up the image of the universe as an area the size of the United States. Imagining Los Angeles to be the far western side of the universe and New York to be the far eastern side of the universe, Earth would fall in somewhere around Kansas City. Our planet would not be visible even through the lens of the most powerful electronic microscope. Bearing this in mind, it is almost inconceivable that this tiny speck is the high point of the entire interstellar intelligence field. Recent estimates by a number of prominent scientists have suggested a probability of at least one million advanced civilizations in the Milky Way alone. Dr. Jastrow, who feels it is feasible though unlikely that we have been visited by extraterrestrial beings, assesses the mathematical odds for the existence of highly evolved societies. Since our galaxy is believed to be about ten billion years old, and Earth is roughly five billion years old, there must be many stars in the galaxy that are billions of years older than our sun. When we reflect on what science has achieved on Earth in this century alone we realize that the advances that could occur in a civilization a billion years older than ours are far beyond the limits of our imagination. Likewise, there must be many worlds that straggle far behind us on the path of technological achievement, but it is chiefly the former who interest us for the vast field of knowledge they might offer us. In assessing which solar systems in particular might be the dwelling places of other humanoid species, we can eliminate those whose suns are larger than ours, for they burn out too quickly to provide the necessary time for the evolution of any complex beings. Solar systems whose suns are smaller than ours would be suitable if they have planets close enough to achieve comfortable temperatures. Stars the same size as our sun, with one or more planets at approximately the same distance from them as Earth is from our sun, would of course make ideal locations. The ten closest stars to Earth known or suspected to have planets or unseen companions within reasonable zones of habitability are listed below with their respective distances from our sun:

Star	Distance from Sun (light years)
Alpha Centauri A & B—a binary star*	4.3
Barnard's Star	5.9
Epsilon Eridani	10.7
61 Cygni A	11.2
Epsilon Indi	11.2
Tau Ceti	11.9
70 Ophiuehi A & B—a binary star	16.7
BD+43°4305	16.9

* A binary star is a system of two close stars orbiting around a common center of gravity.

· 8 ·

INTERSTELLAR TRAVEL

The vast distances involved are what make the concept of interstellar travel at first appear almost ludicrous. They could also be considered one of the most damaging pieces of evidence against the credibility of UFO witnesses. Most people rationalize that if UFO's are not explainable in human or natural terms, then they must be spacecraft of extraterrestrial manufacture. Since many eyewitness accounts indicate intelligent control, the craft would have to be guided or perhaps even occupied by some kind of being. Yet how could living beings traverse the vast regions of space? According to the laws of physics matter cannot travel faster than the speed of light, which in a vacuum is 186,000 miles per second. Merely to reach our closest stellar neighbor a vehicle moving at that velocity would require four years. Perhaps this does not sound too discouraging when we remember the lengthy ocean voyages of the fifteenth- and sixteenth-century explorers, but to date the fastest vehicle man has ever launched travels at a tiny fraction of that speed: 7 miles per second. At this rate it would take a spacecraft eighty thousand years to reach the nearest star.

If, in fact, UFO's are the ships of interstellar travelers who have not transcended the physical limitations of velocity as we know them, it is not inconceivable that they might have developed a method of modifying their life spans. One possibility is through artificial hibernation. Biologists have long sought the secret factor that causes the body temperatures of certain animals to drop to about 1 degree above the temperature of their environment during winter months. During this period all unnecessary bodily functions cease, including growth. If the chemical, enzyme, gene, or whatever could be pinpointed and tapped to induce hibernation in people, then the aging process could be delayed for prolonged periods of time. The alternate route is through cryogenic preservation. This form of suspended animation by actually freezing an organism and later reviving it has already been performed on a minor scale by scientists of this world.

Also to be considered is the possibility of intelligent life in the form of mechanical robots. Perhaps another race might have developed automated servants or replicas of themselves. These machines might advance to the point

Astronaut Edgar Mitchell *(Courtesy NASA)*

where they no longer needed their progenitors. They would have the distinct advantages of memory banks stored with almost limitless information and the ability to make repairs and incorporate new technological developments into their own structures. With unlimited life spans the astronomical distances of interstellar travel would be no barrier to them.

Astronaut Ed Mitchell feels that the evidence is very strong that UFO's do exist but that if their explanation is extraterrestrial visitation, then their creators have learned something about the laws of nature that we don't know yet. In this case he projects that studies in the realm of mental phenomena and the unified or multiple field area will in due course give us the answer. Mitchell thinks it very likely that UFO's come from another dimension. "I am sure," he says, "there is intelligent control somewhere behind them."

Whatever their point of origin, their motivations are perhaps comparable to those of human beings. Of course, it is purely speculative, but it seems feasible that other civilizations might share our basic instinct to explore and cross new frontiers. Perhaps they, too, are forced by expanding populations and diminishing resources to push out beyond their own worlds and see what the universe has to offer.

· 9 ·

INTERSTELLAR COMMUNICATION

While interstellar travel is presently beyond the power of the human race, interstellar communication is not. Dr. Jastrow notes that our initiation of radio communication only sixty years ago must surely have been preceded by thousands if not millions of years on other planets. Their mastery of the technique and ability to transmit signals over great distances probably far surpasses our progress in the field. Several years ago a British astronomer spotted a curious set of markings on the paper graph of her radio telescope. From somewhere in outer space someone or something was broadcasting a signal. The scientific world was alerted. Long investigation revealed the existence of a new kind of invisible star called a pulsar, which sends out radio waves. This time it was from something. Next time it could be from someone.

Project Ozma, the first attempt to detect radio signals from other worlds, was carried out in 1960. It failed. Since then several other attempts, in which the different investigators chose different targets, have met with equal failure. However, the odds for success were very slight indeed. The number of stars that have been investigated is less than .1 percent of the number that would have to be examined if there were to be a reasonable statistical chance of finding one extraterrestrial civilization. Although in 1964 the Soviet Union announced that two of its astronomers had detected signals transmitted by highly developed beings from a planet in the 61 Cygni solar system, American scientists have remained skeptical of this report.

In 1971 NASA initiated plans for Project Cyclops, a system whose design called for a circular array of over fifteen hundred antennas, each larger in diameter than a football field, covering over twenty-five square miles. Although this project would have allowed a more realistic effort to eavesdrop on radio transmissions in outer space, its enormous size and cost made it somewhat impractical. It remained in the planning stage. Yet it seemed there was no other feasible method of intercepting radio communications from other civilizations. Then at the end of 1976 scientists and engineers at the Caltech Jet Propulsion Laboratory designed new equipment of unprecedented tunability and sensitivity. Utilizing existing antennas at the Deep Space Network in Goldstone, California, this equipment can survey the entire visible sky. The project, known as SETI, or the Search for Extraterrestrial Intelligence, may well bring us our first official contact with beings from other worlds.

Meanwhile we have been unintentionally sending messages out into space for the past fifty years or so in the form of commercial radio and television waves. The first of those signals are now 50 light years distant and may already have been picked up by other civilizations. In 1974 man sent out his first deliberate announcement from the Arecibo Observatory in Puerto Rico. The message, composed by Frank Drake, head of Project Ozma and director of the Arecibo Observatory, and Carl Sagan, biologist and astronomer, is a coded signal describing our numerical system, the chemistry of life on Earth, the advancement of man's structure, growth, and brain, population figures, the position of our planet in the solar system, and information about the transmitting telescope. Although the chances are excellent that intelligent beings will intercept this communication since it will reach all three hundred thousand stars of a group called Messier 13 in the Great Cluster of Hercules, Messier 13's distance of 24,000 light years means that it will be at least forty-eight thousand years before mankind receives an answer. This makes the undertaking lose some of its excitement. But perhaps in twenty-four thousand years someone in the Great Cluster of Hercules will be grateful to twentieth-century man for his efforts. Likewise, perhaps we soon will be fortunate enough to receive tidings sent out thousands of years ago by some other society in space.

The only messages to be sent by unmanned space probes are aboard Pioneer 10 and Pioneer 11 in the form of plaques designed by Carl Sagan and Linda Saltzman Sagan. In pictorial scientific language the plaques describe the port of origin and impart basic information about humans. Pioneers 10 and 11 were launched in 1972 and 1973 respectively, on exploratory missions to Jupiter and Saturn. This part of the journey completed, they will travel on and leave our solar system toward the end of the decade. Carl Sagan admits that this form of communiqué could be compared to a shipwrecked sailor placing a message in a bottle and casting it into the ocean. Its best chance of reaching another civilization is for it to be picked up by another spaceship traveling in interstellar space.

Groups of people around the world insist that telepathic communication is already taking place. One of these groups is headed by Don Elkins, a former professor of physics, and his associate Carla Rueckert, in Louisville, Kentucky. They claim that for the past thirteen years,

Above: Artist's concept of the high aerial view of
the entire Cyclops system
Below: View from ground level of Cyclops system antennas
(Courtesy NASA)

during their weekly meditation sessions attended by many of Elkins's former students, they have conversed with and questioned members of a Confederation of Planets who channel their responses through the voice systems of the various people present. The sources of these communications seem, for the most part, to exist as astral rather than physical bodies, although they are capable of adjusting their vibrations to project into our dimension. The messages are of a philosophical and intellectual nature rather than technological. Despite this, their celestial prediction in April, 1974, dealing with an astronomical occurrence, came to pass on schedule in the summer of 1975 in the form of a nova. This prediction is interesting because of the fact that man is unable to anticipate this particular phenomenon. A well-known case of this type of communication reportedly occurred several years ago in Eliot, Maine, where a Mrs. Swann was receiving messages through automatic writing and voice channeling. This experience was apparently shared by her neighbor Rear Admiral H. B. Knowles and two members of the Office of Navy Intelligence sent to investigate. The information given was highly technical. When the interviewers requested to see their contacts, they were told to look out the window, whereupon a shining disk appeared in the sky. We include these reports because we feel that the possibility of telepathic communication cannot be ruled out.

The desirability of communicating with and encountering extraterrestrial civilizations could be considered questionable. Many assume that any society advanced enough to cross the interstellar reaches would have transcended the warlike tendencies of less developed civilizations such as our own. The danger of subterfuge cannot be ignored, however. Seemingly benevolent aliens might use their superior intelligence to subvert us, playing on our ignorance. Even with the most peaceful intentions on their part, the culture shock to our planet could be traumatic.

Artist's conception of Pioneer 11 as it flies past Saturn in
December, 1979, before leaving our solar system.
On board is a message from the people of Earth.
(Courtesy NASA)

We should not be misled by the blind faith of pseudo-
religious cultist groups who, in the words of Dr. Hynek,
"find solace and hope in the pious belief that UFO's
carry kindly space brothers whose sole aim is a mission of
salvation." Still, it is to be hoped that the benefits to be
gained would far outweigh the risks. The transfer of greater
understanding in the fields of medicine, technology,
ecology, culture, and even spiritual development could
bring about a highly rewarding stage of evolution on the
planet Earth.

There is another question, however: Are we already
being visited by extraterrestrials?

PART

Three

A WATCHFUL EYE
ON CELESTIAL OBJECTS

· 10 ·

THE NATIONAL INVESTIGATIONS
COMMITTEE ON AERIAL PHENOMENA

Twenty years ago U.S. Air Force Colonel Joseph Bryan III asked Lloyds of London what odds they would give him on a one hundred dollar bet that the existence of UFO's would be proved by 1965, and on another one hundred dollars that we would establish communication with them. Lloyds would not bet. Yet in 1956 public demand to know the truth about "flying saucers" was so great that retired Marine Major Donald Keyhoe, long a believer in the extraterrestrial hypothesis and angry at the almost conspiratorial way in which the Air Force seemed to be handling the matter, formed the National Investigations Committee on Aerial Phenomena. Colonel Bryan was appointed to the board of NICAP. Although 1965 has passed without proof of extraterrestrial visitation, his conviction that UFO's are real machines remains unshaken. "One of these days," he says, "a UFO *will* land in full view of responsible, unimpeachable witnesses. I hope I'll be among them."

NICAP is headed today by John Acuff, Jr., and includes on its governing board Senator Barry Goldwater and Congressman J. Edward Roush. Not all members of the Board of Governors are convinced believers in the extraterrestrial hypothesis. Board member Brigadier General Robert Richardson III explains,

> While I hold no great belief in the possibility that there is, or ever has been, any extraterrestrial origin associated with the so-called UFO sightings and reports, I am very much interested in early identification of new scientific facts or technologies whether initiated by us or by others. Efforts to explain unexplained events can lead to this directly or indirectly. As such I consider NICAP's effort to replace the USAF in keeping careful watch over reported UFO activities—and seek explanations for these—could contribute possibly to scientific progress and even possibly to national security.

Like Major Keyhoe, some saw in NICAP the means of seriously analyzing a problem that they felt the Air Force had mishandled. Major Dewey Fournet (U.S.A.F., Ret.), an aeronautical engineer, recalls, "Before my association with the official USAF project, I looked on the subject with considerable skepticism. However, shortly after I was assigned to monitor the project at USAF headquarters with the opportunity to examine all the material in the files, my attitude changed." A few years after his release from the Air Force NICAP asked him to become a member of the Board of Governors. He points out that his decision to join was not a hasty one:

> I consented to serve only after I was satisfied that NICAP was dedicated to a serious objective study of UFO's. . . . The USAF project was increasingly assuming the appearance of a travesty. In retrospect, I now believe that the USAF had become convinced that no threat whatsoever to the national security was involved, and they were look-

ing for the right opportunity to dump the project without arousing too much public backlash.

Major Keyhoe has often been accused of being harsh with the Air Force in his opposition to their policy. "I think there's been a terrible blunder the way this subject has been handled by the Pentagon," he says. But he was always aware of the reasoning behind the debunking campaign. "Of course, if I had been on active duty during the early period," he says, "particularly in the Air Force, I would have had to do exactly the same thing: lie about it and knock down every answer and ridicule witnesses. . . ." Keyhoe, too, had initially been a skeptic.

> If it hadn't been for Admiral Farney, a Naval Academy classmate of mine, showing me about two hundred Navy Marine Corps reports of encounters, I would have continued to be skeptical, but I thought, "Gosh, that seems to be quite a full issue." It's hard to believe at first but when you do, then you get kind of peeved at people who won't listen to you.

NICAP's role is not that of upholder of the extraterrestrial hypothesis but rather that of the unbiased investigator. With the assistance of competent people from the scientific community the members aim to follow up every lead a case offers and make every effort to explain erroneous reports and expose hoaxes. Only those cases that remain truly unexplainable are then put down on the record as UFO's. NICAP board member Joseph B. Hartranft, Jr., President of the Aircraft Owners and Pilots Association and founder of the National Intercollegiate Flying Club, also involved in other aviation groups including the Bates Foundation for Aeronautical Education and instrumental in the founding of the Civil Air Patrol, feels that "it is a matter of some importance that NICAP's operations have identified and eliminated from the core of information many hoaxes and exposed many charlatans, whose interest in the phenomenon of unidentified flying objects has been directed more toward commercial aggrandizement than factual research and analysis." Through the years Hartranft has had frequent reports from civilian pilots "in which various experiences have been related concerning objects in the sky which they have often described in detail. These reports have come from many parts of the country—and some foreign—from people unknown one to the other and yet some of the descriptions have remarkable similarity." However, when it comes to defining the nature of UFO's, Hartranft states, "what they may be or even if they truly exist, I have nothing more than an open mind and I think these determinations must ultimately come from the experts in the field of science which is what the whole NICAP program is about."

Research is carried out by regional investigators all over the country. NICAP employs them on a volunteer basis. These investigators must meet certain basic requirements before being approved by the selection committee. Essential qualifications for the position are the necessary background and training to use proper scientific methods of investigation. These involve educational or occupational training in the physical, social, or behavioral sciences, or experience in other specialized fields, such as law, medicine, education, or engineering. Moreover, investigators have to be sufficiently established in their communities to be able to work effectively with law enforcement, government, and other local authorities.

Each month NICAP sends out to its four thousand members a newsletter called *UFO Investigator*. Membership is ten dollars annually and is the main source of funding for this nonprofit organization. Activists in the field lament the lack of government funding. Says NICAP president, John Acuff, "Government funding for Project Blue Book was insufficient for the task and its effective use is highly debatable. Why would one of the most puzzling subjects in the history of mankind lack research funding?" One factor that he feels may have contributed to this absence of proper financing is the "ultra sensationalistic reporting which gave voice to the so called 'lunatic fringe.' The widespread publicity given to reports having a high general interest factor but very low credibility tended to hide the really strong cases from the general public. The natural result of this is that there was no 'grass roots' support for funding and therefore very little funding was approved."

NICAP refrains from involving itself in sensationalism even though this would bring more members to the organization and hence more resources with which to undertake recordkeeping and research. General Richardson feels that the solution lies in bringing together the several major UFO organizations in the United States.

If all these groups continue to compete for the small amount of financial and membership support available to UFO research by responsible scientists—a condition largely attributable to the "kooky" image given the business by past profit and publicity seeking speakers and writers—the entire nationwide effort will suffer as the small amounts available are largely eaten up in multiple overhead costs.

Unfortunately, not all UFO research groups are entirely reliable and unbiased in their investigations. Moreover, there has been a certain amount of discordance between the various organizations, although it is gradually being replaced by more and more co-operation.

Meanwhile NICAP has built up files of approximately three thousand unidentifiable sightings out of fifteen thousand reports. Of these three thousand UFO's, some could be explained if more data were available for analysis, but most of them would remain classified as UFO observations. Although Colonel Bryan would have lost his bet with Lloyds of London, the abundance and strength of the data do prove that something is being seen in our atmosphere that cannot be explained. That "something" seems to be craftlike, is usually disk-shaped, and is solid enough to be picked up by radar. That "something" seems to move in a controlled manner and at speeds and with maneuverability that cannot be matched by any product of our technology.

· 11 ·

INVESTIGATING UFO'S

The first recorded UFO sighting in history was made by the Egyptian Pharaoh Thutmose III more than fourteen hundred years before the birth of Christ. Since then, historical records show evidence of many strange objects, lights, and flying contraptions being witnessed by people all over the world. The Bible contains numerous references to flying chariots, which today some people interpret as primitive man's description of an extraterrestrial spacecraft. In 329 B.C. Alexander the Great told of his army being dived upon by two great shining silvery shields spitting fire around the rims. Other great men who saw or recorded such sights as heavenly disks, spheres, huge lights, and burning shields, were Plato, Aristotle, Pliny, Cicero, Bede, and Charlemagne.

In the United States the first great wave of sightings occurred over nineteen states from November, 1896, to May, 1897. They are generally referred to as "the airship sightings" because their general description was somewhat similar. But the first manmade airships were not developed until several years later.

Today these same things, if indeed they are the same things, are called unidentified flying objects, or UFO's.

There are many problems involved in investigation and

research, not least of which are those generated as a result of the general attitude toward such phenomena. Many witnesses will not come forward to report their experiences for fear of ridicule. Others, who do not stop to think about the reactions their stories will incur, are often greeted with insults and a total lack of co-operation from official agencies. The result of this is that these reports go uninvestigated, and if they do eventually reach any of the qualified investigating groups, it is usually too late to carry out any conclusive research. The attitude of law enforcement agencies is fast changing, but there are still many people who, upon seeing something in the sky that they do not recognize, just do not realize that they should bother to report it.

A major problem in UFO investigation is precisely that we do not know what we are investigating. A police officer investigating a burglary aims to find the whereabouts of the stolen goods and catch the thief. When he achieves this his case is closed. A doctor attending a sick patient must diagnose the illness, identify its cause, and prescribe the appropriate treatment. But what can a UFO investigator do? He can only ascertain the facts; if after he does this the object proves to be truly unidentifiable, then his work ends there. The case is never closed.

The first step a NICAP investigator takes is to seek an explanation for the sighting. This he does by checking with all airports, military bases, governmental installations, research centers, and police stations in the area. If none of these provides a lead he must then ascertain that the object seen was not a natural phenomenon such as a meteor, a satellite, or a large star. If there are photographs of the object, tests are carried out to establish whether or not a hoax is involved. Many of the UFO organizations have hundreds of pictures in their files that blow-ups and density tests have revealed to be frisbees, misidentified conventional craft, photographically superimposed images, lens flares, and so on. But there are some photographs that remain unidentifiable. The most famous are the two pictures of a shiny silver disk taken by Paul Trent, a farmer in McMinnville, Oregon, on May 11, 1950. These photographs are valuable because of the points of reference, namely the barn, the telegraph pole, and the mountains in the background. Studies over a twenty-five-year period have been unable to establish the flying object in the pictures as anything but an unidentified disk-shaped craft. In 1954 a French military pilot took a picture of an almost identical object near Rouen in France. Another series of photographs generally considered as legitimate are those of a disk-shaped craft seen off Trindade Island, Brazil, by mariners on several vessels in the area. Its credibility is supported by the fact that twelve scientists aboard a Brazilian Navy ship testified to having witnessed the craft.

If the investigator is unable to find an immediate explanation for the sighting, he must then attempt to verify the credibility of the witness and his report. Radar is the most conclusive means of confirming a visual sighting but where radar confirmation is not available the investigator must look for other witnesses. Failing this, he must try to find out whether or not the witness has a reputation for truthfulness and reliability.

At this point he collects every scrap of information that the witness can supply, including sketches. An official NICAP report form is completed and mailed to NICAP headquarters in Maryland. A copy of the form is included on pages 92–93. All the information collected from all over the world to date has not helped us to understand what UFO's are, but it has helped us to realize that many people in different places at different times are seeing the same things. The majority of reports indicate disk-shaped objects, cigar-shaped objects, and luminous objects. Other persistent features are the proximity of many UFO's to power stations, the disappearance of some into large

UFO photographed by
Paul Trent in
McMinnville, Oregon
(Courtesy NICAP)

UFO witnessed off
Trindade Island,
Brazil *(Courtesy NICAP)*

bodies of water such as lakes and reservoirs, reactions to them by animals, power failures, stalled car engines, and the presence during or after some UFO sightings of angel's hair, a white gossamerlike material that usually dissipates within hours.

Rarely does an investigator ever see one of these objects himself. Ernie, a former police officer and now a NICAP investigator for the New York area, collects information on dozens of cases year after year, interviews credible witnesses including police officers, pilots, and radar operators, and yet he has never had the ultimate evidence of seeing a UFO with his own eyes. Does it bother him? Yes, it does. He would very much like to see one. But what keeps him going are the facts that there are so many

sound cases with reliable witnesses, that interest in the phenomenon is growing rapidly, and that, as in any other scientific venture, simply because you cannot find the answers immediately is no reason to give up on the whole project.

Ernie's interest in UFO's began when he joined the Air Force in 1955. He worked in the radar and communications center where he encountered firsthand hard evidence on the radar screen. Other bases, too, were picking up UFO's on radar, objects that traveled at high speed, made right-angle turns, and in general did not fit in with the normal traffic patterns for the area. Jets were sometimes scrambled after the UFO's and the pilots returned with strange reports of what they had seen. Often something

NATIONAL INVESTIGATIONS COMMITTEE ON AERIAL PHENOMENA (NICAP) ®
3535 University Blvd. West
301-949-1267
Kensington, Maryland 20795

REPORT ON UNIDENTIFIED FLYING OBJECT(S)

This form includes questions asked by the United States Air Force and by other Armed Forces' investigating agencies, and additional questions to which answers are needed for full evaluation by NICAP.

After all the information has been fully studied, the conclusion of our Evaluation Panel will be published by NICAP in its regularly issued magazine or in another publication. Please try to answer as many questions as possible. Should you need additional room, please use another sheet of paper. Please print or typewrite. Your assistance is of great value and is genuinely appreciated. Thank you.

1. Name   Place of Employment

    Address   Occupation
                                                            Date of birth
                                                            Education
                                                            Special Training
    Telephone   Military Service

2. Date of Observation   Time   AM   PM   Time Zone

3. Locality of Observation

4. How long did you see the object? _____ Hours _____ Minutes _____ Seconds

5. Please describe weather conditions and the type of sky; i.e., bright daylight, nighttime, dusk, etc.

6. Position of the Sun or Moon in relation to the object and to you.

7. If seen at night, twilight, or dawn, were the stars or moon visible?

8. Were there more than one object?   If so, please tell how many, and draw a sketch of what you saw, indicating direction of movement, if any.

9. Please describe the object(s) in detail. For instance, did it (they) appear solid, or only as a source of light; was it revolving, etc.? Please use additional sheets of paper, if necessary.

10. Was the object(s) brighter than the background of the sky?

11. If so, compare the brightness with the Sun, Moon, headlights, etc.

12. Did the object(s) —   (Please elaborate, if you can give details.)

    a. Appear to stand still at any time?   f. Drop anything?
    b. Suddenly speed up and rush away at any time? g. Change brightness?
    c. Break up into parts or explode?   h. Change shape?
    d. Give off smoke?   i. Change color?
    e. Leave any visible trail?

13. Did object(s) at any time pass in front of, or behind of, anything? If so, please elaborate giving distance, size, etc, if possible.

14. Was there any wind?   If so, please give direction and speed.

15. Did you observe the object(s) through an optical instrument or other aid, windshield, windowpane, storm window, screening, etc? What?

16. Did the object(s) have any sound?   What kind?   How loud?

17. Please tell if the object(s) was (were) —

    a. Fuzzy or blurred.   b. Like a bright star.   c. Sharply outlined.

18. Was the object —   a. Self-luminous?   b. Dull finish?   c. Reflecting?   d. Transparent?

19. Did the object(s) rise or fall while in motion?

20. Tell the apparent size of the object(s) when compared with the following held at arm's length:

    a. Pinhead   c. Dime   e. Half dollar   g. Orange   i. Larger
    b. Pea   d. Nickel   f. Silver dollar   h. Grapefruit

    Or, if easier, give apparent size in inches on a ruler held at arm's length.

21. How did you happen to notice the object(s)?

22. Where were you and what were you doing at the time?

23. How did the object(s) disappear from view?

24. Compare the speed of the object(s) with a piston or jet aircraft at the same apparent altitude.

25. Were there any conventional aircraft in the location at the time or immediately afterwards? If so, please elaborate.

26. Please estimate the distance of the object(s).

27. What was the elevation of the object(s) in the sky?   Please mark on this hemisphere sketch.

28. Names and addresses of other witnesses, if any.

29. What do you think you saw?

    a. Extraterrestrial device?   e. Satellite?
    b. UFO?   f. Hoax?
    c. Planet or star?   g. Other? (Please specify).
    d. Aircraft?

30. Please describe your feelings and reactions during the sighting. Were you calm, nervous, frightened, apprehensive, awed, etc.? If you wish your answer to this question to remain confidential, please indicate with a check mark. (Use a separate sheet if necessary)

31. Please draw a map of the locality of the observation showing North; your position; the direction from which the object(s) appeared and disappeared from view; the direction of its course over the area; roads, towns, villages, railroads, and other landmarks within a mile.

32. Is there an airport, military, governmental, or research installation in the area?

33. Have you seen other objects of an unidentified nature? If so, please describe these observations, using a separate sheet of paper.

34. Please enclose photographs, motion pictures, news clippings, notes of radio or television programs (include time, station and date, if possible) regarding this or similar observations, or any other background material. We will return the material to you if requested.

35. Were you interrogated by Air Force investigators? By any other federal, state, county, or local officials? If so, please state the name and rank or title of the agent, his office, and details as to where and when the questioning took place.

    Were you asked or told not to reveal or discuss the incident? If so, were any reasons or official orders mentioned? Please elaborate carefully.

36. We should like permission to quote your name in connection with this report. This action will encourage other responsible citizens to report similar observations to NICAP. However, if you prefer, we will keep your name confidential. Please note your choice by checking the proper statement below. In any case, please fill in all parts of the form, for our own confidential files. Thank you for your cooperation.

    You may use my name.   ( )   Please keep my name confidential.   ( )

37. Date of filling out this report   Signature:

that at first had seemed to be unusual later turned out to be a small aircraft. But during Ernie's four years in the Air Force he was involved in a dozen cases that were considered unexplainable. Official forms were completed and sent in to a base at Colorado Springs. However, the official reports that followed did not seem to bear out the initial accounts by the original witnesses, all of whom were well-trained, intelligent individuals, not likely to jeopardize their military careers by making false and unfounded allegations. Consequently Ernie began to take a harder and more serious look into the UFO situation and several years later joined NICAP, first as a member and then as an investigator. The first outstanding incident Ernie investigated was the Albany case in 1974.

PART

Four

UFO
CASE HISTORIES

· 12 ·

UFO'S STUN
THE CITIZENS OF ALBANY

Up until 1974 Ernie had been involved chiefly in cases where witnesses reported sighting odd lights in the sky rather than close-up, clearly defined objects. These light sightings occur almost daily. The Albany case, however, was different. It was one of the best documented because it involved civilians, police, the Federal Aviation Administration, and military authorities, and was, moreover, confirmed by radar. To this day Ernie still receives letters and phone calls from private individuals and other investigative organizations requesting more information on the case.

On August 20, 1974, at eight o'clock in the evening, a barrage of telephone calls from startled citizens began to hit the Saratoga State Police barracks at Malta as well as local radio stations, television stations, and newspaper offices. The very first caller asked the police if they were aware of any unusual aircraft in the area. When told,

"No," he replied, "In that case, I would like to report an unidentified object over my home."

State Trooper Michael Morgan was dispatched to the caller's address. By the time he arrived he found a police detective, who had been in the area, watching a blimp-sized object, which had now risen to an altitude of about 500 feet and moved out over Lake Saratoga. As they stood there watching the reddish, glowing object flashing on and off almost like a strobe light, two other seemingly smaller objects came in above it. They began to merge with the first object. The bewildered officers, unable to rationalize what they were seeing, felt sure that they had to be helicopters or something similar, and expected at any minute to see some unfortunate aircraft come crashing out of the sky. They called Albany airport and alerted Air Traffic Control Supervisor Robert King, who told them there was nothing operational in that area. The objects merged completely; at this point they were spotted on the radar scanner at the Albany tower, appearing as one target.

After remaining merged for a few minutes the two smaller objects broke away and left in the direction from which they had come. The first object began to move slowly toward the two policemen. As it came over them Trooper Morgan shut off the engine of his patrol car. As they tried to look up at the immense form above them they were so dazzled by the brilliant white light shining out of the center of its base that they were unable to make out its dimension. Then, never making a sound, the craft made a funny little turn, passed almost right over the nearby police barracks, and moved off at a very nonchalant rate. Suddenly it disappeared, "as if," said Morgan, "someone had reached up and turned the lights out. It was that quick."

During this time another trooper, Warren Johnson, radioed in that there was a UFO above the Northway, an extension of the New York Thruway that goes up to

Canada. Morgan and the detective left to join him to tell him of their experience and to reassure him that he was not hallucinating.

Meanwhile, back at the Albany tower, the radar operators had observed what appeared to them as one object splitting into three and moving off in different directions. A pilot flying a small craft in the area was asked if he would investigate. He made two passes over the location but could see nothing in the cloudless night sky. The pilot gave up and landed. After a total 45-minute period from when they had first picked up the target, the radar operators lost all contact with it.

Shortly afterward another odd call came in, this time from the pilot of a military aircraft flying over the Albany area at 8,000 feet en route to Griffiss Air Force Base. The pilot asked the controllers abruptly if there were any high-speed aircraft in the area. To their negative reply he answered, "Well, something just passed us at about one thousand feet over our heads. It looked like a red fireball going by, and it's heading right your way."

Immediately one of the senior traffic controllers went to an end scope that was not in use and adjusted it to its full range of about fifty miles. He caught the object just as it was coming in on the edge of the screen, heading straight for Albany. To make sure that it was not an "angel" (a ghost image caused by temperature inversion where an object reflected on the ground is picked up by radar), he threw the anti-clutter device, but the image still came through sharp and clear. There was no doubt that it was a solid object being tracked. Since GCA (Ground Control Approach) radar does not determine speed the controllers made quick mathematical calculations based on the distance covered and the number of 360-degree sweeps made, each full sweep on the scope lasting four seconds. They came up with a result of 3000 miles per hour. About five miles outside Albany the target

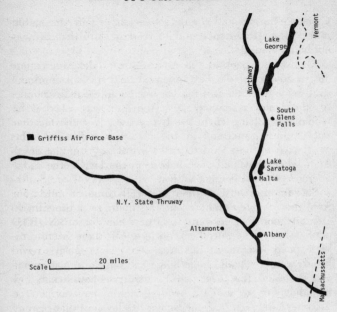

Map showing landmarks of August, 1974, UFO sightings in
northeastern region of New York State

vanished. It was there one moment and when the next
sweep came around it was no longer there.

Ernie discussed the various possibilities with Air Traffic
Control Supervisor Bob King, with his colleagues who
were present at the time, controllers John Guzy and Neil
Parker, and with Data Systems Specialist Tom Esposito.
They concluded that for the object to have come out the
other side of the scope that quickly it would have had to
have picked up a speed of at least 5000 miles per hour;
on the other hand, if it had hit a blind spot on the radar
and gone straight up it would have involved a fantastic

maneuver of which no known manmade craft is capable. The possibility of its being a meteorite is eliminated because at that low altitude a meteorite would have to come down, and if anything that large had struck the ground five miles from Albany it would have made an enormous crater and the impact would have been heard for miles around.

Later reports revealed that almost within the same time frame that night large unidentifiable disks and bright lights were seen moving at a rather low altitude over the South Glens Falls area and as far north as Lake George.

Ernie checked with the Cambridge office of the Smithsonian Institution, which at that time was headquarters for Project Moonwatch, a Smithsonian-sponsored program to link astronomers across the world that has ties into NORAD (North American Air Defense Command) on satellite re-entry and other aerial activities. He asked them to find out if anything unusual in the way of a natural occurrence had taken place that night and their reply was that they were aware of absolutely no natural phenomenon in the area during that time period. They added that if any natural body of such immense size had entered the atmosphere it would have lit up the whole sky like a Christmas tree.

The most startling part of the story was yet to come. During his investigation of the August 20 sightings Ernie was apprised of an unreported UFO occurrence that had taken place just one day before, August 19. Investigator William Goblet of the New York State Police Department telephoned him and told him of an incident involving his own mother. Mrs. Viola Goblet, an employee of the Nash Nursing Home in Altamont, New York, together with the nursing home's director, Mrs. Ruth Currie, had witnessed an object similar in description to that seen by state police in the Albany area the following day. Goblet was adamant that Ernie speak with the nursing home director, who, it seemed, had had previous UFO sightings including one of an actual landing. "Do you know anything about the lady?" asked Ernie. "Yes," replied Goblet. "She's no fool. She worked for the Office of Navy Intelligence during World War II and she's a very honest person. Besides, there were other witnesses, too."

Ernie wasted little time in meeting with Bill Goblet and together they drove to the Nash Nursing Home. Mrs. Currie was glad that somebody was willing to take a serious interest in the matter and explained why she had never reported any of the sightings. Apparently there had been a number of sightings in the area during the past couple of years by many different people. A local journalist had written to Washington requesting some kind of investigation but without result. Mrs. Currie herself had reported a sighting approximately a year before to the local police. "They just laughed right in our faces," she said, "and told us not to worry about it, that it was probably just a logical thing. I wasn't about to be made a fool of twice. I just kept quiet until the last time when Viola saw it too, and she had her son, Bill Goblet, talk with me."

Between the end of April and August 19, 1974, Mrs. Currie had seen a total of five UFO's, usually when she was scanning the sky for shooting stars to show her young daughter, Laurie, who had never seen one. Sometimes she thought she had actually found shooting stars until the "shooting" circular lights, usually bluish in color but sometimes red, would suddenly stop, remain motionless in one spot for a certain amount of time, and then speed off again in another direction.

But it was actually Laurie who spotted the craft in the first of this series of sightings. Between 9:30 and 10:30 in the evening on about April 30 Laurie looked out of the window and said, "Mommy, there's a car up on the road." "Gee, Laurie," said Mrs. Currie, thinking that it must be Kay Thorpe, one of the women who was due to take over the night shift at 11 o'clock, "it's early for Kay to be coming in." "I don't know, Mommy," said Laurie. "Maybe they had an accident up there. There are red lights." Mrs. Currie joined Laurie at the window and together they peered through the darkness at what they thought must be a car parked several hundred feet up the road. "Maybe they're up there making love," said Laurie mischievously. But Mrs. Currie pointed out that the lights were on inside the vehicle and when one parks a car the lights are not on unless the door is open. "In fact," Mrs. Currie said later, "I wouldn't say 'lights.' It was more like a golden glow unlike anything I've ever seen before." The vehicle was straddled right across the road, large enough in fact to be a trailer. But even more than the improbability of a trailer being parked sideways on that piece of road, Mrs. Currie was puzzled by the red lights on the front and the back. She and Laurie decided to take a closer look and, as they stepped outside, they heard the horses whinnying and what sounded like all the dogs in the neighborhood barking and howling. "It was just bedlam," she said. When they were about two hundred feet from the object, they stopped. Now they could clearly see a huge oval object resting on the roadway with red lights at both ends and what appeared to be a large, rounded window on top, emanating a brilliant golden glow. But what really chilled them and stopped them in their tracks was the figure moving about inside the craft. "I stood there for a long time," said Mrs. Currie, "telling myself I was going crazy." They could not make out whether it was a man or a woman, or if it was even a person. No features were distinguishable, nothing was visible in the golden glow except for the mysterious form walking back and forth, bending over and moving around as if working on something. The amazed mother and daughter stood there for a while. Then Mrs. Currie told Laurie to go in and fetch Rose Curtis, an employee of the nursing home. Mrs.

Curtis, as stunned as they were when she saw the craft, ran back into the house and telephoned her husband. Not mentioning anything about a UFO, she simply urged, "Bob, could you get up here, there's something up here and we're afraid." She ran back outside to join Mrs. Currie and Laurie until, finally, realizing that they were not dreaming and that what they were looking at was stark reality, the three women decided to return to the house. As they walked away there was a whistling sound. "Who's whistling?" asked Mrs. Currie of Laurie. Then thinking it was Mrs. Curtis, she turned to her and said, "Were you whistling?" "No," said Mrs. Curtis. For a moment Mrs. Currie felt a chilling breeze but could not be sure if it was caused by her fear or an actual gust of wind. Then a whirring sound made the women turn around. The UFO was gone from the road. It was way up in the air and fast disappearing into the night sky.

When Bob Curtis arrived, minutes later, his wife asked, "What took you so long? What took you so long?" He, too, seemed shaken and said, "I stopped on the way up here. I almost ran off the road." "What are you talking about?" said Mrs. Curtis. "I haven't any idea," he answered. Mr. Curtis explained that as he had approached the nursing home he had seen an object rising very rapidly from the grounds, up over the trees. He screeched to a halt and watched the circular object, with red and blue pulsating lights all around it, as it came toward him, rising all the time. When it reached an altitude of about a thousand feet it stopped momentarily, just sat there for a second or two, and then it was gone. "I haven't any idea how fast it was going," said Mr. Curtis, "but I've never seen anything move that fast in my life. It just disappeared in front of my eyes."

The next day they all went up on the hill to look at the landing site in the daylight. There they found a scorched circular patch about seventy-five feet in diameter.

Where the circle overlapped the lawns on either side of the road, the grass was burned and charred. Within the circumference of the circle were two deep indentations in the road, shaped like half-moons, but without any kind of tread marks. Ernie went with the state police to examine the area with a geiger counter but with the time span that had passed and the intervening heavy rains, there was little evidence left, only a few indistinct marks.

His inquiries of other residents in the area uncovered a large number of people who had witnessed UFO activity on several occasions, but all of whom had been afraid to report their experiences for fear of ridicule by local authorities. It was mere chance that State Trooper Goblet had read about Ernie's investigations of the Albany case shortly after hearing from his mother about events at the Nash Nursing Home. While the lateness of the investigation made it hard to corroborate some of the information, Goblet's telephone call to Ernie did at least disclose an astounding case that otherwise would have gone completely unrecorded.

· 13 ·

CARS DODGE
SWOOPING UFO'S

Ernie investigated another case that year that had gone unreported at the time because the witnesses were unaware of an appropriate place to make such a report. It was only by chance that Frank Pilon, a supervisor at the New York Telephone Company whom Ernie knew personally, happened to mention the incident to a mutual acquaintance who finally relayed it to Ernie.

About 8 o'clock one January evening, Mr. and Mrs. Pilon and their ten-year-old daughter were driving along

Route 31 through Spruce Run, New Jersey, on their way to the nearby town of Washington. Out of the corner of his eye Mr. Pilon noticed three brilliant round lights coming down over the mountains toward the highway. Thinking them to be aircraft with their landing lights on he paid no attention until he realized that they were getting extremely close and that the lights were getting larger and larger. Not wanting to upset his wife and daughter, he said nothing. Suddenly the little girl in the back seat cried out, "Daddy, Daddy, I think those planes up there are going to hit us." Mrs. Pilon said, "Yes, now that she's mentioned it, I've been watching them. They're coming right at us." "All I could see," said Frank Pilon, "were these bright white lights in a triangular formation coming in at us. They came so close that I pulled off to the side of the road so that we could bail out of the car." The two cars behind them did likewise. As the three huge, round craft came in over the Pilons' car, they suddenly broke formation, one of them going straight over the car and up at a very high speed, and the other two breaking east and west. They flew out, regrouped in a layered position, and, making a 45-degree turn, disappeared over the mountain range from which they had first appeared. The Pilons noticed that as the lead object passed over the car, its glow intensified greatly, only to diminish again as it flew off.

When Ernie spoke with Frank Pilon about the incident, he asked him, "I wonder what's out on that highway that

would have brought them in like that! Were you near a reservoir or a power plant?"

"No," answered Pilon. "Why do you ask that?"

"Well," said Ernie, "usually when a UFO comes down like that, there's something that brings it down, like a large body of water or some kind of power source."

"No," said Pilon, "there's nothing in that area."

"Are you sure?" asked Ernie.

"I'm positive," said Pilon.

The next day Ernie called on Pilon at his office to pick up his completed NICAP report form and found Pilon looking a little embarrassed.

"You know," he said, "you were right."

"What do you mean?" asked Ernie.

Pilon explained that the previous evening he had gone home and told his wife, "You know, Ernie says it's funny that there wasn't a power plant or something around there."

"Well, there was," she said. "We were sitting right next to the New Jersey Power and Light Station." The giant electric substation was hidden from the road by a dense line of trees and Frank Pilon had never been aware of its presence.

Ernie was able to determine that there were no weather balloons or aircraft in the vicinity at the time, but because several months had passed between the incident and its investigation, he could uncover no other aspects of this case. The viability of the case lies in the responsible reputation and good character of the witnesses, personally known to the investigator, and in the proximity of the area to a power plant, a feature corresponding to other UFO sighting areas. To this day the Pilons are evidently shaken by their experience and remain perplexed and curious as to what it was they saw that January evening in 1974.

· 14 ·

DOG SENSES UFO

A subsequent case in which delayed reporting impeded
investigation does, however, display some interesting cor-
roborative evidence. On February 17, 1975, Ernie contacted Bob Huber, a newspaper reporter for the *Staten
Island Advance,* to ask him for details on an article he
had written about a UFO sighting reported by two
fifteen-year-old youths in Annadale, Staten Island.

At about 7 o'clock on the cold, crisp evening of
February 10, the two boys were testing the ice on a local
pond to see if it was strong enough to skate on the next
day. To their delight the ice was firm and solid. They
turned to make their way home, and at that moment one
of them caught sight of a huge orange ball glowing
brightly against the backdrop of twinkling stars in the
clear night sky. Without uttering a word, he nudged his
friend, who looked up at the strange football-shaped
object, approximately twenty feet in diameter and only
about four hundred feet away from them. For ten minutes
they watched spellbound, feeling no strange effects and
hearing nothing other than their own heartbeats. Suddenly
they noticed that the outer edges of the orange glow were
beginning to converge upon its center. When it had
shrunk to about the size of a basketball, it vanished into
thin air. The frightened boys hurried home.

The next morning they returned to the pond and found
that several of the trees in the area had been sheared to a
height of about four feet off the ground, trees the width of
a man's neck. Some of them were coated with a black,
carbonlike substance.

For three days the boys kept quiet about their discovery

and then they called the *Advance*. Ernie and Bob Huber went to the pond to examine the scene. There they inspected the trees, finding that they had been snapped off recently, well within the time limit of the boys' experience, for the sap was still fresh and running. But it was definitely not the type of shearing that would have been caused by someone swinging an ax. It was more of a splitting effect, almost as if the trees had been struck by lightning. Nor could the damage be attributed to wind, for it had occurred in a small confined area and the trees around were unharmed and untouched.

Pointing to the black soot, Huber said, "The area's all burned here."

"I don't think this burned," said Ernie. "Take a whiff of the air."

"I don't smell anything," said Huber.

"That's what I mean," replied Ernie. "If these trees had burned, with this wet weather, we'd have smelled it right away."

The black substance seemed to have collected on the trees as if it had been deposited there. They set about collecting dirt and wood samples, which were then submitted to extensive chemical analysis and radiation tests.

The reports indicated that the black residue found on the wood was carbon based and came from a low intensity heat such as the burning of paint thinner or lighter fluid, but chemists found remnants of neither. It has been known for oil-laden wood found around seashore areas to achieve spontaneous combustion under the right temperature conditions and to burn into a glow. But Annadale is far from the water and the below-freezing temperatures that night were far too cold for this type of mineral fire to have existed. The orange color noticed by the observers would suggest a heat of very low temperature such as might be caused by dry brush or weeds burning, but there was no evidence of any such fire. Forensic chemists specializing in arson detection examined the branches and concluded that the fires did not seem to have been intentionally set. In fact, the trees definitely were not set on fire in the normal sense of the word, yet there was some heat source present over a large area of the woods that night that caused carbonization at bark level only, and within a limited area. The gas chromography test was negative. The radioactivity test was negative. The only conclusion the chemists were able to come to was that any of the known causes for such an effect did not apply in this case.

A week later Huber called Ernie to inform him that he had just learned of two more people who had undergone something a little strange on the night of February 17. Danny and Marge Kish, a couple in their mid-fifties, known by Huber to be straightforward and honest people, live only a quarter-mile from the pond. They own a ninety-pound German shepherd attack dog called Rip, who, in Mr. Kish's words, "ain't afraid of nothing!" That night, as he had done hundreds of times before, Mr. Kish securely collared and leashed Rip and took him for his evening walk in the woods. As they drew near the pond, separated from their vision by dense trees, where, unknown to Kish, the two boys were watching the mysterious orange ball, Rip began to whine. He stopped abruptly in his tracks, his whines turning to whimpers and his hackles rising. Suddenly he jumped violently, managing to release himself from his collar—an almost impossible feat—and took off for home in sheer terror. Kish, who had owned Rip since he was a puppy and had had the dog trained specifically to protect him and his family, stood alone in the woods, perplexed.

The next day Mr. Kish's wife telephoned him at work to say that she was worried about Rip and wondered if she should take him to the vet. He seemed to be suffering from heart palpitations, continued to whine and pant, and spent the whole day cowering in his master's armchair, despite the fact that his strict training had always prevented him from jumping on furniture and despite Mrs. Kish's repeated admonitions. He refused to eat any food that day. Rip did not begin to calm down until that evening when Mr. Kish returned home from work, and it was two days before he was completely normal again.

A few years before Kish had seen a UFO over that area but, after one person with whom he spoke asked him if he had been drinking, he decided not to report it for fear of ridicule. On this occasion he naturally did not connect his dog's strange reactions with the presence of a UFO, particularly since he himself had neither seen, heard, nor felt anything extraordinary. He knew nothing of the sighting until a few days later when he read about it in the newspaper. Then he made contact with Bob Huber.

The main problem of investigating the case lay in the fact that the site was not examined until a week after the incident, thus reducing the reliability of the chemical analyses of the samples. Moreover, it is always difficult to research that particular type of phenomenon. When dealing with a light in the sky or a metallic disk it is possible to confirm it through radar reports, air force records, and so forth, but when the object in question may not even be metallic, it is rather hard to track down any supportive evidence.

The value of this case lies mostly in the significance of the dog's reaction. It is most likely that if a person wanted to invent such a story to attract attention, he would include himself in the sighting. He would, as a rule, have reported that he caught a glimpse of a light, or heard a rustle, or that the wind came up, or that he felt faint. But Mr. Kish stated that he was totally oblivious of anything going on and was merely concerned by his dog's failure to act as the protector he had spent so much time and money training him to be.

The only guess that we can make as to the cause of an animal's violent reaction in such cases is that UFO's generate sound waves of a higher pitch than humans can detect. However, this is hypothesis and it may be that UFO's possess some feature that stimulates another sense in animals of which we are completely ignorant.

· 15 ·

AIR FORCE MEN
WATCH UFO MANEUVER

UFO's do not appear to very small groups of witnesses only. That very large numbers of people have on many occasions observed them at the same time is one of the facts that support their reality as an existing and unexplained phenomenon. One such case involving a crowd of at least twenty-five Air Force personnel is on file at NICAP headquarters and was reported by Major Paul A. Duich (USAF, Ret.) who was on active duty at the time.

The sun was setting over the Strategic Air Command Headquarters at Offutt Air Force Base in Omaha, Nebraska. The date was September 8, 1958; the time 6:40 p.m. Major Duich was in the officers' club where he had just ordered dinner. Deciding to spend some time after dinner reading the newspaper, he excused himself from his friend and colleague at the table with him and started to walk out to the lobby of the Visiting Officers' Quarters next door, where newspapers were sold. The sun had disappeared below the horizon. As he crossed the open space between the officers' club and the Visiting Officers' Quarters, something caught his eye. Glancing up toward the west he noticed what appeared to be a short vapor trail in an otherwise cloudless blue sky. Major Duich walked on, but something about that vapor trail disturbed him.

An experienced observer of vapor trails, he instinctively knew that this one was peculiar. Then he did a double take. The so-called trail had transformed itself into a brilliant source of light, similar in quality to a magnesium flare. Major Duich stopped dead in his tracks and watched.

The light was intense and hung motionless. Major Duich later remarked, "Even a short trail shows generation and dissipation as the aircraft moves across the sky." He watched for two or three minutes before calling to another officer, "Hey, what do you make of that?", pointing to the spot in the sky. "Looks like a short vapor trail," answered the other man. Major Duich pointed out that it wasn't moving or growing or diminishing in size. The officer stopped to stare and several others joined them.

By then they decided that this called for a better look. Rather quickly, they all agreed that the light effect was being created by sunlight reflecting on the vapor trail, even though the sun had already sunk below the horizon. As more people joined the crowd, Major Duich hurried in to the office of the Visiting Officers' Quarters and called the Offutt tower. He asked the tower operator to look west, about 30 degrees from the horizontal and tell him what he saw.

"Looks like a short vapor trail. Very odd."

"Vapor trail, my foot! Look at it now."

Major Duich could see it through the window as he talked to the tower operator. The glow was now diminishing and changing to a dull red-orange, and at the same time the fuzzy appearance gradually turned solid, displaying the distinct shape of a pencil or slender cigar. The upper end was blunter than the lower end.

By then all the men in the office were curious and they all stepped outside with Major Duich to join the ten or twenty others who had gathered to stare at the thing. Simultaneously, the crowd of people began looking at each others' faces, perhaps to reassure themselves of the reality of the situation, for as they watched there appeared at the lower end of the object a swarm of black specks cavorting in all directions, looking almost like a swarm of gnats. After a couple of minutes the black specks disappeared.

Then the object, which until then had hung motionless in the same spot, slowly changed from an upright position into a 45-degree angle with the horizon and started moving slowly toward the west. Although there was no sudden change in the coloring, a perceptible color change did take place.

For about five minutes the awed crowd watched as the object continued moving toward the west. Then very gradually it again began to change its angle, slowly turning into a horizontal position and continuing in almost the same direction, now slightly to the southwest. The apparent size of the object was slowly diminishing and the color fading. It resumed an angle close to its earlier 45-degree position and after another five minutes faded completely, blocked from their view by the many miles of hazy atmosphere between the base and the object. The spectacle had lasted about twenty minutes and after the first ten minutes a full colonel had set up a tripod and 35-millimeter camera with color film and taken several photographs of the UFO. At a later date, when asked about it, he denied ever getting any successful exposures.

As soon as the object had vanished, the observers began asking each other what it was they had seen. "I don't know, but I saw something," was all anyone could answer.

The crowd was composed of civilians and Air Force personnel, at least twenty-five of them officers and airmen. Several of the officers were from the Air Force Ballistic Missile Division in Los Angeles. Several others, like Major Duich, were operations personnel engaged in a Strategic Air Command planning session at the time. All except a few of the airmen were seasoned veteran flyers or highly trained missile engineers. Their unanimous conclusion was that what they had observed was no conventional missile, nor was it an atmospheric phenomenon.

Major Duich collected the names of some of the people present, as he planned to report the UFO to the proper authorities. He called the filter center and reported the facts over the telephone in the presence of a fellow officer

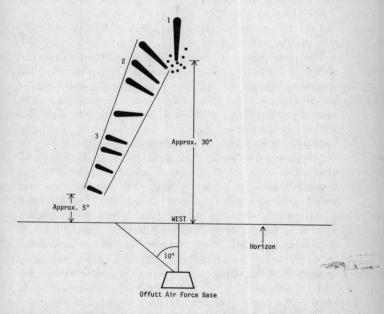

Diagram of UFO maneuvers witnessed at Offutt Air Force Base:
UFO first appeared as a vapor streak, a bright flare of light,
then turned to red-orange, as a solid shape became distinct (1).
Black specks appeared to dance near the lower end. The specks
disappeared as the object tilted to 45 degrees from horizontal
and began to move slowly west southwest (2).
It tipped to horizontal, then, as it moved into
the distance, tilted upward again (3).

and co-worker. He was told that he would be called for an interview within forty-eight hours by the Air Technical Intelligence Center representatives. That was September, 1958. He is still waiting.

· 16 ·

AMERICAN AIRLINES
PLANE TRAILS UFO

In the past, when authorities were not allowed to pretend to ignore UFO reports, they often came up with so-called natural explanations for the sightings, explanations so flimsy that even a child could see through them. One such example was that of a commercial airliner that chased a UFO across New York State.

On April 8, 1956, an American Airlines plane was on its regular flight route from New York to Buffalo with stop-overs in Albany, Syracuse, and Rochester. Captain Raymond Ryan and First Officer William Neff had just taken off from Albany in a northerly direction and were making a left turn when they noticed a very brilliant white light over Schenectady. Thinking that it could only be an approaching aircraft, they began to change course in order to pass to the south of it. But within moments they realized that the object, which was only two or three miles distant, was standing still. They became very curious. As they stared at the object off their wingtip, it suddenly shot into a 90-degree arc turning toward the west, traveling somewhere between 800 and 1000 miles per hour. Ryan and Neff knew that it was no conventional craft, for not only was it too fast even for a jet, but at that low altitude a vehicle would burn up three or four times the amount of fuel it would at a high altitude and at that speed would not be able to maintain a sufficient fuel supply. They called the flight attendant, Ms. Reynolds, who came up to the cockpit and she, too, stared in amazement at the object. It had now settled on a westerly course and was about eight to ten miles ahead of the American Airlines plane. Suddenly the light went out. Ryan and Neff felt a moment of panic. They had a planeload of passengers and something unknown and unseen lay on their course up ahead. What were they to do? They did not move their eyes from the spot where the light had been and, to their relief, almost instantly the light reappeared. But no longer was it white. It had changed to a brilliant orange color. Looking at each other in disbelief, they decided to call Griffiss Air Force Base to see what radar might reveal. Unfortunately the radar was not in use and the operators informed Ryan and Neff that it would take them thirty minutes to energize the set. But they asked the pilots to keep it sighted, to switch on all their lights and keep calling out their location. After the observers in the tower at Griffiss Air Force Base had visually spotted the airliner, they radioed to Ryan and Neff, "The object you see, is it orange in color?"

"Yes, it is," answered the pilots.

The tower controllers called back, "We have a definite silhouette in sight south of the field."

An Air Force man and a Civil Aeronautics Administration man at the Albany tower and observers at Watertown all confirmed visual contact with the UFO. Ryan and Neff were instructed to abandon their next landing at Syracuse and to continue in pursuit of the object while Griffiss Air Force Base prepared to scramble jets after it. The UFO was now traveling at a conventional speed, for the airliner traveling at 250 miles per hour had no trouble keeping it in view. Captain Ryan was beginning to worry a little about holding up his passengers, who had not been advised of what was going on and who were unaware that their landing at Syracuse had been passed up.

He called Griffiss Air Force Base observers, who said they were "about off." Eight minutes passed. They were now too distant from Griffiss Air Force Base and radio communication had to be turned over to the Syracuse tower, which relayed the messages back and forth. Ten minutes passed. The jets were still not off. Twelve minutes passed and Captain Ryan knew that he would have to give up and return his planeload of passengers to Syracuse. The UFO had just passed over Oswego on the southern shore of Lake Ontario, and as Ryan and Neff prepared to turn their plane they saw the bright orange light accelerate and speed across the water toward the northwest, disappearing into the distance.

In 1963 an Air Force "fact sheet" published the following statement regarding the April 8, 1956, UFO sighting: "The Air Force concluded that the object viewed during this sighting was the planet Venus." The control tower operators, experienced, well-trained observers, reported seeing a silhouette of a UFO. The sky that night was overcast. Were the Air Force authorities suggesting that the planet Venus descended below Earth's cloud covering, zoomed through a 90-degree arc, and moved across the sky at a low altitude, changing speed as it did so?

· 17 ·

AIR FORCE JET
INTERCEPTS UFO AND VANISHES

One of the most extraordinary cases, famous among ufologists, where Air Force reports contradict the facts and even their own original reports, involves the loss of an Air Force jet.

On the night of November 23, 1953, controllers at Air Defense Command spotted an unknown target on radar flying over Lake Superior. An F-89C all-weather interceptor was scrambled from Kinross Air Force Base, near Soo Locks in Michigan. Guided by radar, the jet sped northwest across the lake directly toward the object. Ground controllers watching the radar screen saw the F-89 close in on the UFO blip. Then the two blips merged and faded from the screen. From all appearances the aircraft and the UFO had collided. No trace of the jet was ever found nor were the two men on board, pilot Lieutenant Felix Moncla, Jr., and radar officer Lieutenant R. R. Wilson, ever seen again.

The last radar contact with the F-89 showed it to be at an altitude of 8,000 feet, 70 miles off Keeweenaw Point, about 160 miles northwest of Soo Locks. A series of contradictory reports was issued by the Air Force. The original one issued by the Air Force Public Information Office at Truax Air Force Base, Wisconsin, stated merely that contact was lost with the F-89 when it appeared to merge with the UFO. There is no mention of tracking the jet after that. Another report on an Air Force information sheet states: "It is presumed by the officials at the Flying Safety Division of Norton Air Force Base that the pilot suffered from vertigo and crashed into the lake." But no wreckage was ever found and judging by weather reports at the time, the pilot would have been on instruments, in which case vertigo could not have been the cause of any accident. Even had the F-89 not been on instruments at the time, there is no explanation why radar tracked it 160 miles out over the lake and then lost contact just after the blips merged. Later the Air Force issued a new report declaring that the UFO was identified by the F-89 as a Royal Canadian Air Force C-47 and that after the F-89 had identified the "friendly" plane it then turned back to base. The report goes on to say that from that time, "nothing of what happened is definitely known." The Canadian plane was supposedly on a flight plan from Winnipeg, Manitoba, to Sudbury, Ontario. In 1961 Jon Mikulich, a NICAP member, understandably dissatisfied with these statements, wrote to the Royal Canadian Air Force requesting information on the matter. He received an answer from Flight Lieutenant C. F. Page, for the Chief of the Air Staff, Royal Canadian Air Force, stating that "a check of Royal Canadian Air Force records has revealed no report of an incident involving an RCAF aircraft in the Lake Superior area on the above date." Two years later another NICAP member, Neil Almquist, wrote again to the RCAF in an attempt to dig up some further details. The reply he received was even more emphatic in denying any involvement in such an event. The Royal Canadian Air Force's Acting Director of Public Relations, Squadron Leader W. B. Totman, pointed out in his reply that, "Also, as you stated the C-47 was travelling on a flight plan taking it over Canadian territory, this alone would seem to make such an intercept unlikely."

There are two interpretations of what happened over Lake Superior that night of November 23, 1953.

One possibility is that Air Force radar tracked a temporarily unidentified Royal Canadian Air Force plane, the F-89 intercepted it, made the identification, and then crashed for unknown reasons. This explanation, of course, assumes that the fully trained, experienced radar men did not know how to read radar scopes. The Royal Canadian Air Force had no record of such an incident and even if there had been such a flight it would have been entirely over Canadian territory and thus no cause for United States interference. Moreover, because of international identification networks between Canada and the United States, its flight plan would have been known to radar stations and it would have been immediately identified.

The alternative conclusion is that Air Force radar tracked a UFO, the F-89 closed in to investigate, and then collided with or was in some manner destroyed or abducted by the UFO.

· 18 ·

UFO SEEN BY HUNDREDS
IN LOS ANGELES

One of NICAP's most interesting radar cases, because it involved hundreds of visual witnesses and was again confirmation of the incredible speeds achieved by UFO's, was certified by Board Members Reverend Albert Baller, Dr. Earl Douglass, Mr. Frank Edwards, Colonel Robert B. Emerson (USAR), Professor Charles A. Maney, and Rear Admiral H. B. Knowles (USN, Ret.).

On March 23, 1957, at 9:55 in the evening, Mr. K. E. Jefferson of Pasadena saw a brilliant flashing object moving over Downey in the vicinity of Los Angeles. From then on until midnight the police switchboards in the Los Angeles area were flooded with hundreds of calls reporting a UFO.

At the Pasadena Filter Center where reports began pouring in at 11:10 p.m. until 11:50 p.m., the commanding officer, Captain Joseph Fry, notified Air Defense Radar. Captain Fry related that most of the accounts described an orange-red object flashing a bright white light. Some of the callers claimed they heard the "sound of reports" when the light flashed from the object. At the Filter Center itself Air Force Technical Sergeant Dewey Crow and newsman Les Wagner watched the UFO maneuver slowly around the area for over an hour. After the clamor of ringing telephones had subsided for a short while, another call came in just after midnight from Mrs.

Robert Beaudoin, wife of an Oxnard Air Force Base captain. She had seen a large silent object flashing a brilliant red light and maneuvering above the Santa Rosa Valley.

An F-89 interceptor was sent up to locate the object but, according to the Air Force, was unable to make contact despite the fact that at the same time witnesses on the ground could see the UFO plainly near one of the Oxnard runways. Reports continued on into the early hours of the morning with witnesses in various locations describing objects that sometimes hovered and sometimes moved swiftly.

The Civil Aeronautics Administration radar report, obtained later, supplied the conclusive proof that UFO's were flying over the Los Angeles area. At 11:50 p.m. the radar operator noticed a target about fifteen miles northwest and moving northwest. His first thought was that it was a jet. Then he realized that the object was moving much faster than anything he had ever seen on the scope. The radar did not give height of an aircraft, so that he was unable to calculate the UFO's altitude. However, it was not above 10,000 feet since the radar maximum altitude range was about 10,000 feet. About forty miles northwest the target came to an abrupt stop and reversed course, all within a period of about three seconds. It then traveled back along its course again and disappeared off the edge of the fifty-mile limit of the scope. The surprised controllers were still wondering what could have executed these incredible movements when, about five minutes later, two more targets appeared and disappeared off the screen in the same direction as the first. A minute or so later the excited controllers watched yet a fourth target appear in the same area as the other three, ten or fifteen miles northwest, and disappear off the northwest edge of the screen. Taken so completely unawares by the first target, they had not been able to figure out its exact speed but by the time the next blips appeared they were able to clock them. The last three targets had all covered a distance of twenty miles in thirty seconds. The UFO's were traveling at a speed of 2400 miles per hour.

· 19 ·

PAN AM PILOTS WATCH DISKS MANEUVER IN FORMATION

Groups of UFO's are often seen to fly in precisely controlled formations and the fleet seen on July 14, 1952, if the witnesses' calculations are correct, traveled at a speed even more amazing than most estimated UFO speeds.

That evening a Pan American Airways DC-4 airliner flying at 8000 feet was approaching the Norfolk, Virginia, area en route to Miami. The senior captain was back in the cabin and Captain William B. Nash, temporarily acting as First Officer, was at the controls. Third Officer William Fortenberry was in the righthand cockpit seat. The night sky was clear and visibility unlimited. Norfolk lay about twenty miles ahead, and off to the right they could see the glittering city lights of Newport News. At about 8:10 p.m. Nash and Fortenberry noticed a red brilliance in the sky, seemingly beyond and to the east of Newport News. The light quickly became distinguishable as six bright objects streaking toward the plane, at an altitude of about 2000 feet, a mile below them. The six craft were fiery red. "Their shape was clearly outlined and evidently circular," Captain Nash stressed. "The edges were well defined, not phosphorescent or fuzzy in the least." The upper surfaces were glowing red-orange.

Within seconds they could see that the disks were holding a narrow-echelon formation, a slightly stepped-up line tilted to the right from the pilots' point of view, with the leader at the lowest point and each following craft successively higher. The diameter of each disk was about one hundred feet. As the two men stared aghast at the startling sight, the leader suddenly seemed to decelerate. The second and third objects wavered slightly and almost passed the leader. When the line of disks was almost directly beneath the airliner and slightly to the right front, their brightness diminished slightly and they flipped on edge in unison, the sides to the left of the plane going up and the glowing top surfaces facing right. In this position the pilots were able to see that the UFO's were shaped rather like coins. Though the bottom surfaces did not become clearly visible, Nash and Fortenberry had the impression that they were unlit. The exposed edges, also unlit, appeared to be about fifteen feet thick, and the top surface seemed to be flat. While in this edgewise position the last five slid over and past the leader so that the echelon was now in reverse order and still tilted. Then, flipping back into a horizontal position and resuming their former brightness, they darted off in a direction that formed a sharp angle with their first course, their sequence being as it was when the pilots had first spotted them.

Almost immediately Nash and Fortenberry caught sight of two more identical but brighter craft as they darted out from under the airplane at the same altitude as the other six. As the two additional disks joined the formation, the lights of all eight blinked out, then came back on again. Still in line, the eight disks sped westward, north of Newport News. They climbed in a graceful arc above the altitude of the airliner and then blinked out one by one, but not in sequence.

Captain Nash and Third Officer Fortenberry radioed a report of the sighting to be forwarded to the Air Force. The next morning at 7 o'clock they were telephoned by Air Force officials and told to come for questioning. The interrogation was carried out by five men, one in uniform and the others displaying identification cards and badges of Special Investigators of the United States Air Force. They were questioned for an hour and forty-five minutes in separate rooms and then for about half an hour together. Their accounts and all sketches and track charts matched. The investigators told them that there had already been seven other reports including one from a lieutenant commander and his wife. They had described a formation of red disks traveling at high speed and making immediate direction changes without turn radius.

When asked to assess the speed at which the UFO's were traveling, Captain Nash described how they made their calculations.

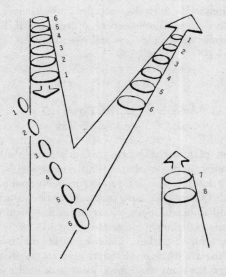

Diagram showing maneuvers of disk formation
observed by Pan American Airways pilots

The objects first appeared about ten miles beyond Newport News. . . . They traveled to within about a half-mile of our craft . . . changed direction, then crossed the western suburban edge of the town areas, out over a dark area at least ten miles beyond the lights, then angled up at about forty-five degrees. We drew a line through the lighted area, measured the distance from our aircraft (and we knew our exact position both visually and by VOR navigation using an ILS needle) to the line through the lighted area. The distance was twenty-five miles. We had seen them cross this line twice, so we knew they had traveled at least fifty miles. To get a time, we seven times, separately, using our own panel stopwatch clocks, pushed the button, mentally went through the time, even to saying to ourselves again, "What the hell's that!" Each time we came up amazingly close to twelve seconds. To be conservative, we increased it to fifteen seconds. Fifty miles in fifteen seconds equals *twelve thousand miles per hour.*

· 20 ·

PASSENGER SEES UFO BELOW AIRLINER

The number of pilots who see UFO's is truly staggering. It is the policy of the various airline companies, however, that their pilots should not report or make public such sightings. UFO witnesses have erroneously been considered mentally unbalanced, morally irresponsible, or prone to hallucinations. Obviously passengers would not feel safe if they thought that their lives were in the hands of someone with these characteristics. However, in private get-togethers, the conversation of pilots turns all too often to their UFO experiences.

One might wonder why airline passengers rarely see

UFO's. This could be partially explained by the restricted area of vision through small cabin windows. Then, too, passengers do not have to concentrate on what is going on outside the plane. Very rare is the passenger who spends the entire trip watching the sky, the clouds, and the terrain below.

But occasionally passengers, too, are the surprised witnesses of strange unknown vehicles. Such was the case of Robert D. Hahn, a jewelry designer, en route from Minneapolis to Los Angeles aboard Western Airlines flight 61 on November 11, 1957. His case might have been less credible had it not been that four engineers on the ground saw strange aerial objects within a few hours of his sighting.

Mr. Hahn was sitting on the right side of the plane next to the window just over the leading edge of the wing. A little while before, the captain had announced that they were flying at an altitude of about 14,000 feet. They now had another thirty to forty-five minutes left before landing at Los Angeles International Airport. The other passengers were busy in conversation or reading. Some had dozed off. Mr. Hahn was gazing out of the window watching several jets making vapor trails at high altitude, crossing and crisscrossing. He looked down at the California desert below. The earth seemed rugged and desolate with no sign of roads or cultivation except for what seemed to be a dirt road meandering about ten to twelve miles to the right, angling away from the plane's line of flight. Looking eight to nine miles ahead of the plane and to the right, Mr. Hahn saw a hill scattered with dark patches that he figured must be brush or small trees. He was puzzled to see a large building at the foot of the hill, a roughly elliptical, metallic structure. He wondered what it was doing there out in the middle of the desert with no roads or other means of access. Suddenly it moved. He saw that the scrub trees were actually passing beneath the huge object as it went up and over the hill angling toward the road. Its course was erratic, seeming to zigzag 200 or 300 feet in an instant to the right or left while maintaining a general direction that was at an angle of about 45 degrees away from the plane's course. The surface of the UFO was not shiny; it reminded Mr. Hahn of sand-blasted aluminum. It was about 200 to 250 feet in diameter and its height off the ground between 200 and 1000 feet. He saw no trail or exhaust from the object and guessed that its overall speed was about a third that of the airliner. All too soon for the curious Mr. Hahn, the craft disappeared from his view behind and under the wing, paralleling the road about a mile to the right. He sat back in his seat wondering what on earth he had seen.

Later that afternoon four Rocketdyne engineers were driving in a generally east-southeast direction from the Rocketdyne SanSu facility toward Canoga Park on the outskirts of Los Angeles. It was 4:20 p.m. and the late afternoon sun was behind them. One of them happened to look up and saw three shiny objects crossing their path from the northeast where the desert lay, and traveling toward the southwest.

"Hey, look at that!" he said to the others.

All four men stared at the UFO's traveling in a V-shaped formation. One was a large, narrow, oval object, almost cigar-shaped, silvery on top, but bright orange underneath. They realized that the orange coloring might be the reflection of sunlight. The two smaller objects were slightly oval, like disks viewed at an angle, and were solid silver in color. One of them was slightly ahead of the large UFO and one of them slightly behind it. Keeping the same positions relative to each other, the three UFO's accelerated and climbed away into the distance.

The four men compared notes and arrived at a consensus that the UFO's were first seen at an altitude of

10,000 feet, climbing to 30,000 feet at an estimated 5000 miles per hour.

Whether one of these objects was the same as that seen by Mr. Hahn, we can never be sure. But the time and the place were close. In fact, these sightings were only two in a wave of sightings that swept the world during that month. It was referred to as the "November, 1957, flap." There have been several of these "flaps" during recent decades. In this one as in the others, many of the reports can probably be dismissed as mistaken identification by overenthusiastic people desirous of being involved in the excitement. But among those reports studied by NICAP there were at least 118 cases occurring in November, 1957, that could not merely be dismissed as attributable to public hysteria. Nor could they be accounted for by manmade aircraft or natural phenomena. There is no doubt that in November, 1957, something was going on in our skies that to this date cannot be explained in conventional terms.

· 21 ·

UFO'S AND THE CLERGY

NICAP has on record several cases of UFO sightings by clergymen, who make up one of the categories of what are considered reliable witnesses.

On February 20, 1952, Reverend Albert Baller of the German Congregational Church witnessed three UFO's similar to those seen by the four Rocketdyne engineers mentioned in the preceding chapter. His report follows.

[It] was an exceptionally beautiful day at Greenfield, Massachusetts. There were no clouds and the sky was a cobalt blue. Also, no wind. At 3 o'clock p.m., I boarded the New York train at the Greenfield station, took a seat away from the station and near a window opening onto a vast expanse of sky to the north and east. A minute or two afterward my attention was drawn to the sky by a sharp flash of light about 35 degrees or more above the horizon. Looking carefully toward this flash, I was quite astonished to see three perfectly circular silver objects approaching in V-formation.

They moved without vapor—or smoke—trail and at approximately the speed of a second hand on a watch. At this speed and in this formation they came to a point almost overhead but not quite, since I could still watch them from my window. There they stopped and hovered for perhaps ten seconds. Then I noted that the lead object was slowly reversing and appearing to pull into line with the other two between them. After this brief shift there was another quick motion by all three (I am not sure just what) and they began to depart in a direction at right angles to their approach.

My astonishment increased as I saw them leave because they went with such speed that they dwindled to specks and were out of sight in not more than six seconds. . . .

Reverend Jack Sanford of the First Congregational Church was with a group of people who saw a football-shaped UFO on October 9, 1960, in Longpoint, Illinois. Reverend Sanford reported to NICAP that they were driving when they first observed the UFO and stopped the car to watch it. When the object began to move after about ten minutes, they attempted to chase it for about three and a half miles until it became a tiny speck in the distance that eventually disappeared altogether.

A pastor of the Grace Lutheran Church in Cleveland, Ohio, managed to get a rather close look at an unknown craft that he, too, attempted to pursue.

The date was November 5, 1955. Shortly after 6 o'clock

in the evening the Reverend Kenneth Hoffman and his wife were driving down Lee Road on their way to the Cleveland-Hopkins Airport. They had just crossed Fairmont Boulevard when, in the dim light of dusk, their attention was caught by a row of bright lights in the sky directly ahead over Lee Road. The lights approached on an arc course and then stopped. As Reverend and Mrs. Hoffman drove on across North Park and Shaker Boulevards, they kept their eyes on the lights, trying to speculate what they might be. At a point on the south side of Shaker Boulevard they stopped the car to get a better look at the strange illuminations, now only half a mile distant. They were able to make out that the lights were coming from a huge oval craft, similar in appearance to two saucers, the uppermost inverted and resting on the edges of the lower one. Around the portion of the perimeter visible to the Hoffmans were eight large windows from which shone an intense white light. It was this light that they had first seen. The UFO appeared to be metallic and was light gray in color, similar to weathered aluminum. The Hoffmans estimated its diameter to be about a hundred feet since it filled the sky above the highway beyond the width of the street. Each window was about eight by ten feet in size and clearly defined, as were the two-foot-wide dark spaces between them. An intensely white beam of light shone steadily downward from each window at about a 45-degree angle. The light rays were so bright that they could see the air dust in them.

Dumbfounded, the couple watched the UFO for about ten minutes, then started the car and drove south on Lee Road, hoping to get under it. As they reached Fernway Road, the UFO began to slip westward over the tree tops, moving slowly and noiselessly, without any apparent rotation. It disappeared from their view behind the tree line.

The Reverend and Mrs. Hoffman discussed what they should do. "We decided," said Reverend Hoffman, "it would be best to keep the matter to ourselves since we felt it might have certain undesirable repercussions if it were made public, our principal concern being the possibility of ridicule and disparagement." As time passed, however, they heard and read of other people who had seen strange lights and craft in the skies. The Hoffmans realized that the time had come to speak up and they told their story in an interview with a NICAP representative.

· 22 ·

RED BEAM SWEEPS GROUND

Certain features of UFO's are repeated over and over again in various reports from all over the world. One such feature is a beam of light, often red, that shines down from some UFO's and sweeps the ground below.

During a six-day concentration of sightings in northern California between August 13 and 18, 1960, which included at least fourteen police officers among the numerous witnesses, a UFO emitting a red beam was seen by State Policemen Charles A. Carson and Stanley Scott while patrolling near Red Bluff.

Ten minutes before midnight on August 13 the two officers were on Hoag Road, east of Corning, searching for a speeding motorcyclist when they saw what looked like a huge airliner dropped out of the cloudless night sky. The craft was very low and directly in front of them. They stopped abruptly and leaped from the patrol car to get a better view of what they were sure was going to be an airplane crash. From their position outside the car the first thing they noticed was an absolute silence. Still assuming it to be an aircraft with power off, they continued to watch. The object was about 100 to 200 feet off the ground when suddenly it reversed completely, at high speed, and gained an altitude of approximately 500 feet. There it stopped. By now the object was clearly visible to both men. It was shaped somewhat like a football, about 150 feet long and 40 feet high, was solid rather than transparent, and emitted a white glow that surrounded the whole object. Red lights glowed from each end and at times about five white lights became visible between them.

The UFO moved again, and Carson and Scott could hardly believe their eyes as they watched it perform amazing aerial feats. It seemed capable of moving in any direction: up and down, back and forth. At times its movement was very slow. At times it was completely motionless. Several times it changed direction or reversed itself while moving at incredibly fast speeds.

The patrolmen pulled themselves together and radioed the Tehama County Sheriff's Office requesting that they contact the local radar base. The radar operators confirmed that their scopes revealed an unidentified radar return at the same location as their visual observation.

Scott and Carson continued to watch the UFO. They made several attempts to get closer to it but each time the craft moved away from them—it almost seemed aware of their presence. They realized they were better off remaining stationary. Twice the object came directly toward the patrol vehicle, causing radio interference. Each time it approached, it turned and swept the area with a huge red light. Officer Scott turned the red light on the patrol car toward the UFO and it immediately retreated from them. Six or seven times the red beam came on, sweeping the ground and sky areas. There were no other aircraft visible.

Eventually the object began moving slowly in an easterly direction and the patrolmen followed at a respectful distance. As they reached the Vina Plains Fire Station, they saw a similar object approaching from the south. It moved near the first UFO and both stopped, remaining in that position for some time, occasionally emitting the red beam. Finally both objects disappeared below the eastern horizon.

Carson and Scott looked at their watches. They had been observing the strange spectacle for approximately two hours and fifteen minutes. They returned to the Tehama County Sheriff's Office, where they met Deputy Fry and Deputy Montgomery, who had gone to Los Molinos after calling the radar base. Both had seen the UFO clearly. The night jailer, too, had observed the object for a short time and had marched his several prisoners out onto the roof of the jail to witness the event. The two deputies and the night jailer described the craft and its maneuvers exactly as Scott and Carson had seen them.

In a letter dated September 16, 1960, to a NICAP member, the Air Force stated: "The findings [are] that the individuals concerned witnessed a refraction of the planet Mars and the two bright stars Aldebaran and Betelgeux. . . . [Temperature inversions] contributed to the phenomena as the planet Mars was quite low in the skies and the inversion caused it to be projected upwards."

In a letter dated October 6, 1960, to NICAP, the Air Force stated: "It is an impossible task to determine what the exact light source was for each specific incident, but the planet Mars and the star Capella were the most probable answers for these sightings."

The change of identification occurred about the time that NICAP reported, in a special bulletin for October, 1960, that the first three named astronomical objects were all below the horizon at the time of the sighting. As it happens, the star Capella was the only one named that was above the horizon at the time.

The State of California was on Daylight Saving Time (P.D.T.) from April 26 to October 25, 1960. The object first appeared at 11:50 p.m. (P.D.T.) on August 13. At that time the planet Mars was about one hour, that is about 15 degrees, below the eastern horizon. It is absurd to suppose that it could in any way account for the sighting. Aldebaran did not rise until about 1 a.m., Betelgeux about 3 a.m.

As for Capella, which was barely above the horizon when the sighting began, no star, by the wildest stretch of imagination, could give the appearance of a large ellipse a few hundred feet off the ground, with red lights at each end and white lights in between. Nor could it cast a beam of red light or maneuver as described by the police officers. Moreover, the objects disappeared below the eastern horizon at the end of the sighting, whereas Capella would have risen about 35 degrees in that period. And, again, this ridiculous interpretation completely ignores the fact that the UFO sighting was confirmed by radar.

Officer Carson's patient reply on hearing such explanations was:

I served four years with the Air Force. I believe I am familiar with the Northern Lights, also weather balloons. Officer Scott served as a paratrooper during the Korean conflict. Both of us are aware of the tricks light can play on the eyes during darkness. We were aware of this at the time. Our observations and estimations of speed, size, et cetera, came from aligning the object with fixed objects on the horizon. I agree, we find it difficult to believe what we were watching, but no one will ever convince us that we were witnessing a refraction of light.

· 23 ·

ANGEL'S HAIR

One of the most extraordinary phenomena occasionally linked to UFO sightings is the white gossamerlike substance known as angel's hair, which has been observed falling from the sky, sometimes in great quantity. However, it has been associated with UFO's in only about half the cases, many times descending from the sky without any prior or subsequent reports of UFO sightings. Frequently in these cases the fibers have been discovered to be nothing but cobwebs spun by spiders, but on those occasions when scientific examination has ruled out the possibility of mold or animal origin, angel's hair has often turned out to be some unidentified kind of plasticlike substance. Unfortunately, though, analysis of the fibers is usually made impossible by their fast dissipation before there is time to get them to a laboratory. Witnesses describe seeing angel's hair dissolve into a gelatinous material, which then dissipates without a trace.

In cases involving UFO's observers usually describe a cloudlike formation surrounding or under a cigar-shaped UFO, from which the angel's hair falls. Strands from a few inches to over a hundred feet long have been reported floating down and settling on the ground or ocean surface.

A sample case is that experienced by a trained biologist, Craig Phillips of the United States Fish and Wildlife Service. One day in 1957 Phillips, then curator of the Miami Seaquarium, was taking part in a specimen collecting trip aboard the Seaquarium vessel, *Sea Horse*, which was skippered by collections director Captain W. B. Gray and his assistant Emil Hanson. They were traveling northward after a successful day's collecting, somewhere between Soldiers Key and Key Biscayne and approximately three miles off the Florida mainland. The sky was clear. The air was still. The three men began to notice occasional strands of what appeared to be very fine cobwebs up to two or more feet in length drifting down from the sky. For two hours the weblike strands continued to waft downward, occasionally catching in the boat's rigging. Gray and Hanson asked Phillips what the webs could be. He explained to them that many natural history books describe how very young spiders, upon hatching, will frequently pay out long strands of silk from their spinnerets until the wind catches them and they eventually become airborne, sometimes being transported many miles and even far out to sea on occasion. Phillips assumed that some phenomenon of temperature or timing had resulted in the mass hatching and exodus of a certain type of spider somewhere on the mainland, and that furthermore, these webs must be fragments of the original strands, which themselves may have been of considerable length. He knew that spiders can at times produce vast lengths of web material at little expense to their own metabolism, and he visualized the little spiderlets, wherever they were, continuing to emit their silken trails during their airborne journey as the wind broke and blew the first ones away. A certain percentage of these strands would be almost certain to have spiders still attached to them, but when the three men caught a number of them on their fingertips no spiders were to be found.

Deciding to examine the substance under his laboratory microscope when he reached the Seaquarium, Phillips carefully placed several of the fine strands inside a mason jar, allowing them to cling to the inside of the glass before capping it. Under high power he hoped to see the tiny droplets that adorn most but not all spider webs, which would leave little doubt as to their true nature. When Phillips reached his office he opened up the jar. It was completely empty. There was not a single trace of the weblike material.

Phillips, a long-time expert on the biology of spiders and their webs, says, "This phenomenon is to me still unexplained, and I have seen nothing comparable to it before or since." He goes on to say, "I would say that it is possible that the strands we saw were something other than spider web, and I have no explanation for the apparent disappearance of the collected material in the mason jar."

· 24 ·

AIR FORCE PRESS CHIEF REVEALS TRUTH ABOUT WASHINGTON UFO'S

Albert Chop, former Press Chief for the United States Air Force and former Information Officer for NASA, has contributed a report on the sensational Washington, D.C., UFO sightings of 1952. Although the news media buzzed for days with the excitement of those events, the story was dropped like a wet fish following a press conference in which a well-presented but specious explanation was put forward by officialdom. This report, published here for the first time, follows the investigation further than the press bothered to go. Chop's general remarks on UFO's and the official reaction follow:

Concerning whether these things could be from another dimension, it sounds improbable, but I don't know enough to do anything but conjecture. It is an interesting speculation, along with the occult ideas. But personally I'd rather go along with the interplanetary theory. While our scientists (some of them) rule out interstellar travel, they really don't know what we ourselves will be doing in one hundred years, five hundred years, or one thousand years from today.

I also believe the Condon Report was and is a deliberate attempt to quiet the public, and I have always believed that was pretty poor public relations. I think it has hurt the Air Force, the Intelligence groups, the rest of the military and the government in general. I remember Gerald Ford, as a congressman, demanding the Air Force release more information to the public. He instigated a Congressional meeting on the subject. How come he did not take the lead after acceding to the most important post in the United States?

The 1952 sightings took place on two nights, one week apart. Al Chop's report on the first sighting follows:

To fully understand the reports of UFO's that were observed electronically and visually on the night of July 26–27, 1952, we need first to recognize that a similar electronic and visual observation had taken place exactly one week earlier, on the night of July 19 and 20. The location of the electronic observance was the same in both cases and many of the personnel involved experienced both sightings.

Location was the FAA Air Traffic Control Center at Washington National Airport. This radar scope was located in a building about a quarter of a mile from the airport control tower. In the tower itself, FAA flight controllers monitor and direct aircraft maneuvers during landings and takeoffs from the airport.

There were three radars involved in both cases. These were:

1 / The radar set in the airport control tower. This is used to direct aircraft on final approach and/or takeoff from the airport.

2 / The radar equipment at the FAA Air Traffic Control Center. This equipment was located in a separate building approximately a quarter of a mile from the tower. This radar set reaches out for long-range surveillance of air-

Albert Chop at Mission Control Center in Houston, Texas, during the Gemini 5 space flight *(Courtesy NASA)*

craft up to approximately one hundred miles from the Capitol area, directs this traffic and then hands control over to the tower if the planes are coming into National Airport.

3 / The military radar equipment located across the Potomac River at Andrews Air Force Base in Maryland. This equipment is used by the military to direct traffic using the Andrews runways. Two Air Defense Command fighter squadrons were normally based at Andrews to

guard the Capitol area, but on the two nights in question these jet fighters were based in Wilmington, Delaware, because the runways at Andrews were undergoing repairs. For security reasons, this was not public knowledge.

On the night of July 19 and 20, shortly after midnight, the flight controllers in the Air Traffic Control Center picked up on their radar scope a number of "unknown" targets, in addition to the routine known aircraft flying in the vicinity.

Senior flight controller James Barnes made a hurried check with controller Howard Cocklin who was in charge of the tower radar. Cocklin confirmed that the tower was also tracking "unknowns." He also told Barnes that he could see one of the targets through the tower windows. "It's a bright orange light, but I can't see whether there is anything behind it," he reported.

Barnes then contacted the military radar control at Andrews Air Force Base. The flight controllers there said, they, too, were tracking the "unknowns."

According to the report of this sighting, several civilian pilots on commercial aircraft also reported seeing "lights" in the sky. Some ground personnel reported similar "lights" were visible.

Barnes and his crew at the control center stated the "unknowns" were observed through most of the early morning hours and that they disappeared at about 5 a.m.

As usual the Press received word of this, and the morning papers carried page one stories about UFO's over the Capitol.

Exactly one week later an almost identical replay took place, except that the "unknown" targets appeared on the radar scopes a little earlier in the evening, shortly after 9 p.m. Al Chop describes his personal involvement in the affair as follows:

I was awakened about midnight on July 26 by a telephone call to my residence. The caller was the FAA Public Information Officer in the Washington FAA office (I can't recall his name). My home was in Alexandria, Virginia, a few miles from the Washington National Airport.

The FAA Public Information Officer told me the Air Traffic controllers at the airport were again tracking a large number of UFO's over the Capitol area. He said the tracking had begun about 9 p.m., and that shortly thereafter the word had spread to the news media. He told me a large number of news people "are beating our doors down." He asked that I come on down to the airport to take over the situation. (Release of UFO statements was the responsibility of the Air Force. I was the official Air Force spokesman for the project at the time.)

I told him that I would be right over. Before dressing I placed a call to Major Dewey Fournet (current Intelligence assigned to Project Bluebook at Air Force Headquarters) at his residence and briefed him on what was happening. He said he would meet me at the control center.

After dressing hastily, I drove to the airport, arriving there about 12:40 a.m., July 27. During the drive I repeatedly glanced skyward. It was a relatively clear night with some drifting clouds. I saw nothing, although the FAA Public Information Officer had also mentioned that some airline pilots and ground personnel had also reported "bright lights" in the sky.

Upon arrival at the control center, I spoke briefly with the gathering of news media people and said I would try to have an Air Force statement for them shortly. All the wire services were represented and in addition we had people from the local papers, the radio and TV stations, several magazine people and a photographer.

I entered the radar room. The scope was approximately

two feet in diameter, circular. It had a phosphor-coated glass top, with a pale blue glow. Traveling around the scope was a large clocklike hand which is called a "sweep." The room was darkened for easy reading of the scope.

After identifying myself to the senior traffic controller, James Barnes, I went over to the scope with him. There were several other traffic controllers huddled around. On the scope several known air flights were being tracked. These were identified by small plastic markers with the flight numbers written in pencil. In addition to this usual known traffic there were a number of similar targets which were marked as "Unknowns." There were from six to a dozen or more of the "unknowns" at various times.

These "unknowns" would appear suddenly in different areas of the scope. They would move on a well-defined flight path exactly as an aircraft would behave. The exception was in their rapid movement. The scope "sweep" circled the radar-scope at a rate of six times per minute.

The "unknown" targets moved too fast for an airplane, although the "blip" or target they cast on the scope was otherwise similar to our known flight aircraft.

The movement of these "unknowns" was sometimes also haphazard. That is, they would move along a definite path for a period of time and then suddenly disappear. Others would as suddenly appear in various places on the scope. Others would remain visible to us for long periods of time.

Barnes had been in voice communication with Andrews radar controllers and with the tower operators. We maintained this communication throughout the night, checking targets on a continuing basis. We were all convinced the three radars were all tracking the same objects.

At approximately 1 a.m., Major Dewey Fournet arrived at the control center. He had picked up an Air Force radar specialist on his way to the airport. This officer, after studying the radar scope, declared the targets were "real solid" and his opinion was that the targets represented solid objects.

While this was going on, I had placed a call to the Command Post in the Pentagon. The Command Post is a Department of Defense (DoD) office which is manned twenty-four hours a day. It has the responsibility for taking charge of military activities in any emergency that may arise suddenly. The Command Post is headed by an officer of Flag rank (or General) at all times. I explained our situation and requested they send an intercept mission from Wilmington. I then turned the phone over to Major Fournet and he urged that an intercept mission be flown. He reported that our Air Force radar specialist had termed the targets "solid returns." Fournet was advised to stand by for an intercept attempt.

At this time (approximately 2 a.m.) I advised our news media visitors that they could take a look at the radar scope, and that we were awaiting an ADC intercept mission. *Life* magazine requested permission to photograph the scope. I had no objection to this, but before they could set up their gear we were alerted that our intercept mission was airborne at Wilmington.

So, I ordered the *Life* camera and the newsmen from the radar room, explaining that an intercept mission would be using classified codes and that I had no authority to waive the classification. The *Life* newsman became incensed at this and told me I would be out of a job on Monday. I said, "So be it, but you can't stay in this room."

With the controllers, Fournet, the radar specialist, and myself huddled over the scope, and just as the flight (two airplanes) became visible on the radar, our unknown targets completely vanished. We were astounded, because the targets had been in evidence throughout the past several hours.

Senior controller James Barnes took over voice contact

with the military pilots. He took his cues from Major Fournet. He split the flight, sending one airplane north and the other south of the Capitol, after informing them that our unknown targets had all disappeared.

We kept them in the area for approximately ten minutes but then released them for lack of targets. They started to leave the area and we watched them disappear from the scope. At the exact moment when we lost contact with them our unknown targets again descended on our scope. It was frightening.

Andrews Air Force Base and the tower controllers also reaffirmed the return of the unknowns. Time was now approximately 2:30 a.m.

Major Fournet immediately phoned the Command Post and informed them of what had transpired. He strongly urged another intercept attempt. He was again told to stand by.

At approximately 3 a.m., we were alerted that the intercept was airborne at Wilmington. About twenty to thirty minutes later the ADC airplanes again became visible on our radar scope. This time our 'unknown' targets remained in view.

Barnes again split the flight on Fournet's suggestion. One to the north, the other airplane to the south. He worked in vain attempting to guide the aircraft in the northern sector to our visible targets. The pilot reported he could see nothing. Barnes then worked with the aircraft flying to the south of the city. At first the same negative results.

Then Fournet pointed out a cluster of about six unknown targets in the south sector. Barnes gave the pilot the compass readings. This aircraft had been designated "Red Dog 2." The pilot to the north had been designated as "Red Dog 1" for intercept purposes.

"Red Dog 2" suddenly reported . . . "I see them now. They are directly ahead of me. They appear to be tremendous white lights, blue-white. They are all around me now . . . They appear to be closing in on me . . ." (This conversation was spread over about five minutes.)

In the control room we had followed the flight of Red Dog 2. We saw his blip moving toward the cluster of "unknowns." We saw his approach and observed that the "unknowns" appeared to place themselves in a ring around his aircraft. We just looked at each other.

"Red Dog 2" then stated . . . "They appear to be moving away now . . ." On our scope it appeared the targets were indeed moving away from his aircraft. Then the pilot reported, "They are gone now, I can't see them anymore."

Fournet requested a description of the "lights" from the pilot but he couldn't add anything to his "blue-white lights" report. He flew around again for a minute or so and then reported that he was returning to base because of his fuel situation.

By this time it was approximately 3:45 a.m. We watched Red Dogs 1 and 2 on their journey back to base. Our unknown targets were also visible. The aircraft faded from our radar range.

We continued to watch the maneuvers of our "unknown" targets, checking various ones with the Andrews radar personnel.

I had jotted down the air-ground communication from the pilot designated "Red Dog 2." I looked over my notes. Major Fournet made a verbal report to the Command Post.

We advised the news media of what had transpired during the intercept attempts, stating merely that one of the pilots involved reported that he had visual contact with what appeared to be large white lights. We affirmed that the "unknown" targets had remained on the scope throughout the second intercept try and told them we hoped to have an official explanation or statement after the Air Force had time to analyze the happening.

In the radar room the "unknown" targets stayed visible

until the early morning hours. They seemed to disappear about the time dawn came. It was approximately 5 a.m.

I left the airport and went to my office in the Pentagon. There I transcribed my notes and routed the transcription to the Command Post, with a copy to my immediate superior, Lt. Colonel Richard Searles, and went home to catch up on my sleep.

The next day the news media headlined the story and the public showed a tremendous reaction. By Monday morning the Pentagon communication lines (telephone and wireless) were completely deluged with demands for additional information.

Captain Ed Ruppelt (Project Bluebook at Wright Patterson Air Force Base) had arrived Sunday night and was on hand on Monday. Major Fournet, Ruppelt, and myself tried to put together a coherent factual report for the news media but that wasn't enough.

The press demanded a conference with top Air Force officials. Under pressure from all sides, Major General John Samford, Chief of Air Force Intelligence, agreed to hold a press conference. It was scheduled for July 29. With General Samford were Air Force specialists on radar, high-ranking officers from the Information Department, and weather specialists.

General Samford gave some opening remarks concerning the continuing efforts of the Air Force to look into the UFO situation because it was their responsibility to do so.

He said the Air Force had been able to satisfactorily explain 80 percent of the UFO reports and that he felt if additional information could have been obtained on the remaining 20 percent, they, too, could be explained to his satisfaction.

General Samford said the Air Force believed the unknown targets observed over Washington were the result of a temperature inversion on both nights. He used several weather and radar specialists to help explain how radar equipment can pick up reflections of ground objects during a period of temperature inversion.

He said many other reports of UFO's had proved to be misinterpretations of conventional objects such as birds, balloons, aircraft, ballooning spiders, etc. He convinced most of those newsmen present that the Washington radar contacts were due to unusual weather aloft over the area.

About one week later, Major Lewis Norman, Jr., an Air Force radar specialist, told Major Fournet, Captain Ruppelt, and myself that the temperature inversion present in the Washington area on the nights in question was not sufficient to cause the radar to pick up reflections of ground objects. Major Norman was a specialist working with the Air Force Aircraft Control and Warning Branch. He said an inversion on the order of 10 degrees to 17 degrees Fahrenheit was required before the radar would react to ground clutter.

The U.S. Weather Bureau figures for the two nights in question showed the temperature inversion present over Washington to be not more than 1 degree on the Fahrenheit scale.

This information was not released to the press. The news media seemed satisfied with General Samford's explanation.

· 25 ·

UFO'S HAUNT ENFIELD

The repetition of sightings in one vicinity is by no means unusual. In early 1975 Ernie investigated one such case, which occurred in rural Enfield, Connecticut. The first sighting took place on February 24 at about 9:50 p.m.

Paul Rogers was driving home along Weymouth Road. About half a mile from his home he caught sight of a huge object hovering at about 60 feet over a field to the left of the road. He slammed on his brakes just in time to avoid running smack into the back of a car that had just stopped in front of him. The drivers of both automobiles stared through their windshields as the silhouetted object, about sixty feet long, hung there over the line of trees that surrounded the field. Paul Rogers was able to make out the form of two large platelike shapes, one inverted over the other, the space between them lit by red, green, and blue rotating lights. It was only about two hundred yards away from him. No more than thirty seconds had passed when the object suddenly disappeared faster than his eye could follow.

The two drivers drove on down the road and pulled off at the first convenient spot. The other driver, a well-dressed, middle-aged man, stepped out of his car. Paul walked over to him.

"Did you see what I saw?" asked Paul.

"Yes, I saw it," answered the man.

"What should we do?" asked Paul.

"Not a thing. I'm going to get back in my car and I'm going to get out of here and go home, because nobody's going to believe what I saw."

Paul said, "Well, I saw it and I believe it."

The man replied, "So that makes two of us!" Telling Paul that he was going to forget that he had ever seen it, he returned to his car and sped off into the distance.

His nerves badly shaken and at the same time overcome with curiosity, Paul continued on home. He could not just drop the experience and went over every detail again and again with his family that night. As Mrs. Rogers listened, she did not realize that there might be a connection between her son's tale and the strange behavior of the family dog at about 9:50 p.m. that evening. Later she explained to Ernie that usually if something bothers the dog, if he hears something, he goes over to the front window, looks out, and barks. That evening, however, at about the same time that Paul was witnessing the UFO, the dog awoke from his sleep in the middle of the living room floor, haunched his body, raised his ears and began to growl very quietly. Then he stopped and that was the end of it.

A short distance from the Rogerses' home, a police sergeant had been watching television. At that time he did not know that what he had seen on his television set earlier that evening might be a sign of something peculiar happening in the neighborhood. He, too, had been momentarily distracted at about 9:50 p.m. As he relaxed in front of his television, the picture on the screen had faded and become scrambled. When the picture reappeared a few moments later he thought no more about it until questioned some time later by Ernie.

Exactly eight days later, on March 4, at about the same time of evening, 9:30 p.m., another car was driving down Weymouth Road. This time the passengers were John Foy, a police officer's son, and his sister-in-law, Joan Pelletier. As they passed the field where Paul Rogers had seen the UFO, they, too, were amazed to see what appeared to be a huge oval object hovering at about 200 feet over the field. For about half an hour they watched the silent craft as it descended toward the ground and then moved off slowly in an easterly direction at about 5 miles per hour.

In a state of great agitation the two witnesses made their report to the police. John Foy seemed particularly upset by the event. Asked to make individual sketches of what they had seen, both tried to recreate their impressions on paper. While John Foy drew an oval object with four white lights in front of it and one red light in the rear, Joan Pelletier's sketch was of a round object with red, green, and blue lights rotating around it. She was, in fact, unsure of the actual shape of the object since the evening darkness had made visibility difficult, but her impression of the lights coincided with those seen by Paul Rogers eight days previously. While John Foy's overall description was similar to that of Paul Rogers, it was in details such as the positioning and color of the lights that he differed. When asked by Ernie if he thought what he had seen might have been a helicopter, John Foy replied no, but that a military helicopter had flown by during the sighting. Ernie was surprised that he could be so sure that it had been a military helicopter. Foy explained that the helicopter was green and that they were not far from Bradley Field.

On the night of April 20, during Ernie's investigations, he received a call at 11 o'clock at night in his hotel room from the desk officer of the Enfield Police Station. The officer told him that at that moment there were six police officers observing a bright object in the sky that they could not identify.

A police unit was dispatched to take Ernie to the scene, but unfortunately the object disappeared before his arrival. In the meantime the desk officer had called Bradley Field to inquire into the possibility of their being any military craft in the area. Bradley advised him that they had nothing operational at that time.

The six police officers described the object as being about the size of a golf ball and at an altitude of about 2000 feet, in a north-northwesterly direction from them. It appeared to make a short up and down movement. It was, they said, a red light with an accompanying white light that pulsed on and off at intervals, and they had observed it for a full forty-five minutes. In compliance with a request Ernie had made earlier for photographs to be made if possible in future sightings, a unit had been dispatched with a high-powered camera but had not arrived in time to photograph the object.

The next day the police station received a telephone call from a local resident asking if there had been any reports of UFO sightings in the area, as she herself had seen one the night before. Ernie went to the caller's home

Field visited by UFO's twice in 1975, in Enfield, Connecticut

accompanied by the Enfield police. She requested that her identity be kept confidential, as she wished to avoid any publicity. Her home was directly in line with the UFO and the point in which the police officers had been standing during the incident. She told them that she and her two sons had watched the object through the living room window for about an hour and a half and her description was exactly the same as that of the police. Ernie asked her if she had ever witnessed that type of phenomenon before. "Yes," she said, she had seen the same object on two other occasions in the same location in the past couple of months.

Ernie then checked with Westover Air Force Base and Barnes Field in neighboring Massachusetts, which both lie in the direction in which the sightings were reported. The reply was that no reports of any sort had been received from radar or local citizens.

Next he called an observatory in Massachusetts and spoke with Mr. Fowler, the director. Mr. Fowler confirmed Ernie's suspicion that based on the direction and the time, the planet Venus could very probably have appeared in the night sky at that time in the manner described by the police officers. Later, information from other observatories corroborated Mr. Fowler's statement that certain atmospheric conditions could cause such an aberrant visual appearance by Venus.

Although no definite identification was possible, Ernie felt that, based on the astronomical evidence and the fact that one of the witnesses had seen the object on prior occasions in the same place, more credence should be given to this object being the planet Venus than a UFO.

As to the February and March sightings, in his final report to NICAP headquarters Ernie concluded that in the case of Paul Rogers the behavior of the dog and the television did not necessarily lend strength to the case, but because they occurred at the same time as the sighting, were certainly worth considering. In evaluating the second incident he felt that both witnesses did observe something that evening which to date is unexplainable. However, after checking with military and private installations in the area, they were unable to account for the helicopter that flew by. Ernie was a little puzzled by Foy's identification of the helicopter, particularly since in the pitch darkness that hangs over the fields of Enfield at night it would be difficult to make out any color, especially at that distance. Nor did any helicopter pilot report anything unusual in the sky that night, but in this case a simple explanation would be that since the lights of the UFO were toward its underside, a craft flying overhead would probably not see them. The weakness in the accuracy of the descriptions led Ernie to feel that perhaps the excited state that the witnesses were in during and after the incident may have caused them to make statements based on what they thought they saw there (such as a military helicopter, which is very common in that area) rather than on what they actually remembered. The book is still open on these cases.

· 26 ·

UFO RESCUES
ARMY HELICOPTER

Only three days after a UFO was witnessed by Ohio Governor John Gilligan and his wife, another incident occurred near Mansfield, Ohio, on October 18, 1973.

Army Captain Lawrence J. Coyne and his three-man crew took off from Columbus, Ohio, at 10:30 in the evening on a helicopter trip to Cleveland. They had no inkling that this was to be the most unusual flight of their military careers. Traveling at an altitude of 2500 feet, they found themselves over the Mansfield area in forty minutes. Suddenly Staff Sergeant Robert Janacsek spotted a red light on the eastern horizon. After watching it for a few moments, he realized that the light was heading straight for them. He warned Captain Coyne, who immediately took over control of the helicopter and put it into a 20-degree dive at 2000 feet per minute. As they reached 1700 feet, the object was zipping down toward their right side. Coyne was scared. There was no time to take any further action. He braced himself for the impact.

Just as the collision seemed imminent, the object came to a stop about 500 feet above the aircraft. The helicopter was still headed downward on its evasive course. Hearts beating, Coyne and his crew looked up through a stream of green light that flooded through the bubble canopy of the helicopter and turned everything inside green. They saw a big, gray, metallic-looking hull about sixty feet long, shaped like a streamlined fat cigar. There was a red light on the front. The leading edge glowed red a short distance back from the nose. A dome protruded at the center. The green light was cast by a swiveling spotlight at the rear.

Captain Coyne got on the radio and tried to contact Mansfield Airport. The radio would not transmit or receive. He realized that the helicopter must be getting dangerously close to the ground and that he had to pull it out of the dive. He hoped it was not too late. With the green light still illuminating the helicopter, Coyne looked at the instruments. He was shocked to see the needle of the altimeter rising. All controls were set for a 20-degree dive, yet they had climbed from 1700 to 3500 feet with no power in a couple of seconds and were still rising. The four men felt no G-forces or other noticeable strains, nor was there any noise or turbulence.

After only a brief moment they felt a bounce and the UFO took off to the northeast. After seven or eight minutes radio contact was reestablished.

Although Philip Klass, the great skeptic of ufology, suggests that what the helicopter crew saw was actually a fireball, it seems difficult to imagine four trained military men making such an elaborate misidentification. When one considers that the altitude of that part of Ohio is 1300 feet above sea level and that therefore the helicopter was only 400 feet above the ground and on a downward trajectory, one is left with the impression that perhaps someone or something deliberately saved that helicopter and its crew from almost certain destruction.

· 27 ·

POLICE RADIOS JAMMED
AS UFO PASSES OVERHEAD

On July 12, 1975, Ernie was called to the town of Parsippany, New Jersey, by the Deputy Chief of Police, Arthur
Denny. Lacking any formal programs of procedure in the
event of sightings of strange aerial phenomena, Denny
needed some expert assistance in investigating the peculiar
events that had occurred in the neighborhood on July 4.

Thursday evening marked the beginning of a long holi-
day weekend. Tom Cahill, a political science major at
Boston College, had taken his girlfriend, Jane Tiger, to
see *The French Connection* at a movie theater in Paramus.
Toward midnight traffic was thinning out. Much of the
population had already settled down for the night, ready
for the day of celebration ahead. Five minutes after midnight, as Tom Cahill and Jane Tiger found themselves
driving home with the last stragglers on Route 46, Cahill
noticed an odd configuration of very bright lights moving
slowly just above tree-top level on the left of the highway.
At first he thought he was watching an airplane coming in
at a low altitude, but there was something about those
lights that bothered him, that made him think it was not
an airplane. He could not quite put his finger on it. Later
he realized that although the lights had been shining
directly at them and greatly illuminating the surrounding
area, there had been no glare whatsoever from them.
Moving in a southwesterly direction, the huge, silent object
moved gracefully toward them at a speed of about 5 miles
per hour.

Traffic on Route 46 slowed down to a crawl. Cahill,
looking up with his head out of the window as he drove

directly beneath the object, had the feeling of passing underneath the hull of a ship. The metallic base of the craft was completely smooth and without marks, and close enough so that if it had been a helicopter he could have read the serial number. Its diameter between sixty and eighty feet, the craft covered the whole width of Route 46. Cahill figured that in relation to its total mass the object might have weighed about thirty tons. Shaped like a squat submarine, it had dull blue-green and red lights at each end, with two small white lights on one side. From the top protruded a turret or dome lit by a very pale, almost translucent, green light. Jane Tiger described it as "the weirdest color I ever saw. It didn't have a quality like our colors." At first they thought that the turret was spinning but soon realized the spinning effect was an optical illusion created by the metal bars spaced one foot apart that surrounded the turret.

As the UFO pulled across the highway, a bright white beam of light appeared, sweeping the land below and giving the impression that it was looking for something or attempting to land. As it hovered overhead at about 75 feet, Tom Cahill pulled over into the parking lot of a diner on Route 46 to get a better view. Within seconds the object changed its angle slightly and then whizzed off, disappearing faster than the eye could follow.

Meanwhile, at police headquarters in Parsippany something strange was going on. The radio communications system had gone haywire between headquarters and patrol cars in and around the Parsippany section of Route 46. At 12:05 a.m. units outside the area were able to hear both sides trying to communicate. Their messages were being transmitted but neither side was able to hear the other. Then at approximately 12:30 a.m. the problem cleared up of its own accord.

Shortly afterward Tom Cahill and Jane Tiger came into the station. They had already reported their odd experience to the nearby Mountain Lakes Police Headquarters, but their story had not been treated too seriously. At the Parsippany–Troy Hills station desk officer Lieutenant John Walsh listened to them quietly and took down all the details.

Although at first the Mountain Lakes police officers had considered the young couple's story rather silly, they had second thoughts and decided to do some checking. Since the location of the incident was not in their township, they called up the neighboring Denville police station, which dispatched Patrolman Rick McConnel to the area. The Denville police had also been experiencing radio interference in the same time frame, but not as severely as the Parsippany unit had.

Upon receiving the call from the dispatcher, Patrolman McConnel proceeded from the center of town to the location of the sighting. At the Route 46 intersection he was forced to stop for a red light. He looked around but observed nothing unusual. Then, easing the patrol car forward until it was jutting out onto Route 46, he was able to see three lights suspended over the parking lot of a restaurant. They were about ten feet higher than the top of the building. The two upper lights were steady. The lower one was rotating. McConnel could not make out any structure in the darkness. After a few seconds the configuration of lights began to gain height and headed over the top of the restaurant in an easterly direction. It passed over some trees toward a group of buildings and came to a halt at the far side of one of them. The lights remained stationary for only a few seconds before dropping downward out of view. Patrolman McConnel did not wait for the traffic light to turn green. He pulled out onto Route 46 and sped eastward. He searched in vain for the strange object, but there was no sign of it. He parked his patrol car in a parking lot and waited in the hope that it would reappear. Another police sergeant, also responding to the

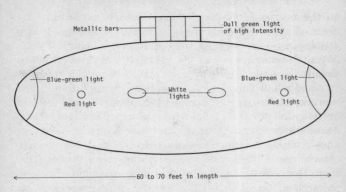

Sketch of UFO seen in Parsippany, New Jersey

call, drove up. When McConnel explained what he had seen, the sergeant gave the embarrassed patrolman an odd look and drove off. After fifteen minutes had passed McConnel gave up. He was puzzled. It was almost as if the UFO had vanished into the lake that lay beyond the buildings.

When Ernie questioned Tom Cahill and Jane Tiger on July 12, they told him that a reporter from the local newspaper had interviewed them. The reporter had mentioned an unconfirmed report that a private pilot flying out of Caldwell Field, New Jersey, had observed a similar object later that day. Police Chief Ellwood Fox then instructed his men to attempt to locate the pilot. He made a request to the local newspaper to run a small article requesting any residents who had witnessed any unusual objects in the same time period, especially the pilot of a private aircraft who might have witnessed it, to get in touch with the Parsippany–Troy Hills Police Department at their earliest convenience.

On the same afternoon that the article appeared, the

Parsippany police began to receive phone calls from residents in the area. One of the first calls was from a Mr. Jim Quodomine, the pilot they had been seeking.

Jim Quodomine, a private pilot with six years' flying experience and an engineer for WOR Radio, had spent the evening of July 4 with his fiancée, flying around over the area observing the fireworks display. He had landed at Caldwell Field at about 10 o'clock that night. They were tying down the small Cessna 150 plane when a couple with a young child came onto the field. They asked Quodomine if there was anyone on duty in the tower. The tower was closed until the following morning, he told them, but seeing that they were a little distressed, he asked if he could be of any help to them. They asked if he knew of any large objects in the air that evening that might have resembled the Goodyear blimp in size. He knew of nothing.

Then the man pointed up to the sky and said, "Do you see that light over there?"

Quodomine looked up at the large white light sitting low in the night sky. "It's too close to be a star," said Quodomine. "It's very bright. It's probably an aircraft."

"Well that thing's been up there for about an hour now," said the man. "It came in low over our car down on the highway. At first I thought it was the Goodyear blimp. It was huge and had a spinning turret with white and green lights." The large craft had moved off from them at a rather high speed, climbing up into its present position, where it had been sitting motionless for the past hour. The couple had stopped at the field in the hope that the tower could identify the object for them.

Quodomine said to his girlfriend, "Do you want to see what it is?" "Yes, let's take a look," she said. They untied the Cessna 150 and took off again. After climbing to an altitude of 3000 feet, they began to close in on the object. As they came to within four or five miles of it, they were able to make out the outline of the craft and the lights that had been described. Realizing what he might be witnessing, Quodomine attempted to close in as fast as possible on the craft. He had the throttle wide open but, unfortunately, wide open in a Cessna 150 is only about 100 miles per hour. He was a little nervous but he had to know what it was. His girlfriend, her anxiety growing, said, "Maybe we ought to turn back?" In her fright she was momentarily convinced they were going to be whisked off to some other world and that she would never see Earth again. Quodomine tried to allay her fears. As they approached within three miles of the object, its lights suddenly changed intensity. It began to move off at high speed and within seconds had disappeared from view. The Cessna 150 was alone in the sky. Dejectedly they returned to Caldwell Field. The couple who had alerted them was gone. There was no one to discuss it with, to try to figure out what it was they had chased. Quodomine was still frustrated by the experience several days later when he read the newspaper article requesting assistance. He responded immediately in the hope that someone might be able to give him an answer.

Of course, he never did get an answer. Nor did the numerous witnesses who logged reports with the police department and with NICAP. Oddly enough, nothing was ever heard from the couple who had first pointed out the UFO to Jim Quodomine. It is possible that they were just passing through the area on their way to another state and thus were never aware of the subsequent investigation. With luck, they may read this book and say, "Hey, we were that couple," and come forward with their information.

Ernie and Detective George Klaus of Parsippany reflew the route of the chase with Jim Quodomine, and photographed the landscape. A rural area with several deep lakes and reservoirs, the terrain is predominantly flat and open, providing many locations for a large craft to come down and be totally undetected by passing vehicles and pedestrians.

Warner Electronics was called in to check out the police communications system. As a matter of fact, they had checked the system less than two weeks before, when a similar disruption had occurred for a very short time. On neither occasion was there any defect found in the radio system. The only recourse was to run over the possibility of outside interference. But checks with the FCC, airports, and local authorities, carried out with the assistance of State Senator James Vreeland, proved negative. There was nothing in the area capable of blanketing out ultra-high frequencies.

The incidents in Parsippany and Denville in July, 1975, heralded the beginning of a series of sightings in various parts of New Jersey throughout the rest of the year. The sightings continued into the new year and in February a new rash was reported to the Parsippany–Troy Hills Police Station by what NICAP considers sincere and credible witnesses. Things have been quiet there now for several months, although in other parts of New Jersey and New York sightings are being reported continuously. Have the UFO's left Parsippany for good or is there something there that will bring them back? It may well be that the many lakes and reservoirs in the area are the attracting feature. In over 50 percent of reported sightings UFO's are seen going into, coming out of, or near water. Says Deputy Chief of Police Arthur Denny, "I've noticed after reading up on reports from other parts of the country, that so many of the sightings occur near water. We have so many lakes around her. They've been seen by the Wanaque Reservoir, the largest in the state, and by the Jersey City Reservoir, and Lake Hopatcong. It seems to be standard operating procedure for them."

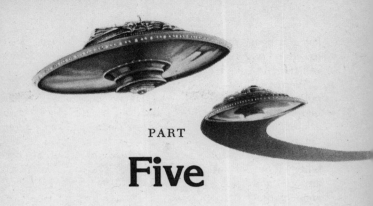

PART

Five

THE CHANGING ATTITUDE
TOWARD UFO'S

· 28 ·

UFO'S AND
THE AIR FORCE

"By what right can we summarily ignore their testimony and imply that they are deluded or just plain liars?" says Dr. J. Allen Hynek of UFO witnesses. "Would we so treat these same people if they were testifying in court, under oath, on more mundane matters?" The answer is no. The humiliating treatment afforded to some witnesses is inexcusable, although publicity-seeking hoaxsters and unbalanced pseudo-religious cults may be partially blamed for the skepticism toward UFO reports in general.

The modern UFO era was ushered in on June 24, 1947. Kenneth Arnold, an Idaho salesman and private pilot, was flying near Mount Rainier, Washington, when he spotted nine "peculiar-looking aircraft" without tails, which flew in a chainlike line and swerved in and out of the high mountain peaks. In his account to newsmen at the time, Arnold described the objects as flying as a saucer would if you skipped it across water. The dubious term "flying saucer" was born. Its connotation did not augur a serious, scientific outlook on the phenomenon.

A wave of UFO sightings that followed throughout 1947 gave rise to the fear that new aircraft or secret weapons were being tested by an enemy in preparation for another war. The United States Air Force was called in to investigate the reports and to determine whether or not they constituted a threat to the national security. Their involvement began in early 1948 with Project Sign, later renamed Project Grudge. It continued in 1952 with Project Blue Book and ended in 1969 with the Condon Report, an Air Force/taxpayer-sponsored study conducted at the University of Colorado.

Since all the interesting reports were in the hands of and classified by the Air Force, the scientific community was prevented from conducting studies of its own. Thus the Air Force's controlling hand in investigating reports led to the controversial atmosphere of secrecy. When Project Grudge issued its final report, it made an effort to provide explanations for all of 244 cases. Not only were some explanations reportedly highly speculative, but 23 percent still remained unidentified. In one sweep the report brushed off these remaining cases as being psychologically motivated since there was no other readily available explanation. With Project Blue Book, the Air Force decided that since UFO's were not a threat to national security, UFO *reports* were, and their aim was to educate the public to this fact. Two members of Condon's team, David Saunders and Norman Levine, shattered any belief there may have been in the impartiality of the investigations when they made public a memorandum written by Project Coordinator Robert Low shortly before the project was initiated. Excerpts from the memorandum read:

> Our study would be conducted almost exclusively by nonbelievers who, although they couldn't possibly *prove*

a negative result, could and probably would add an impressive body of evidence that there is no reality to the observations. The trick would be, I think, to describe the project so that to the public, it would appear a totally objective study, but, to the scientific community, would present the image of a group of nonbelievers trying their best to be objective, but having an almost zero expectation of finding a saucer. One way to do this would be to stress investigation, not of the physical phenomena, but rather of the people who do the observing—the psychology and sociology of persons and groups who report seeing UFO's. If the emphasis were put here, rather than on examination of the old question of the physical reality of the saucer, I think the scientific community would quickly get the message. . . .

It is premature to have much of an opinion, but I'm inclined to feel at this early stage that, if we set up the thing right and take pains to get the proper people involved and have success in presenting the image we want to present to the scientific community, we could carry the job off to our benefit. . . .

Condon immediately fired Saunders and Levine for insubordination. His final summary of the investigations ignored many of the conclusions made by other contributors to the report and reflected, for the most part, his personal views.

The termination of Air Force involvement in 1969 brought about declassification of UFO records. However, researchers did not have access to the files. Only if a researcher knew of a specific case by name and date would the Air Force then pull that particular case file. But the worst blow to researchers came when the Air Force offered the records of Project Blue Book to the National Archives. To protect witnesses' anonymity, restrictions on the release of material included the deletion of names of witnesses and all other identifying data, investigators' conclusions, confidential sources of information, and investigative techniques. Since the enormous budget and manpower required for such a task rendered it impractical, the records remained inaccessible for some time. It was only after dozens of requests were filed under the provisions of the Freedom of Information Act that a private company was commissioned to complete the task. On July 12, 1976, the records were finally made available to the public, but the deletion of so much pertinent data has diminished their value to the researcher.

· 29 ·

UFO'S AND THE U.S. CONGRESS

Despite the fact that the Air Force debunking program succeeded in convincing some people of the supposedly spurious nature of UFO reports, there were those who remained disturbed by the phenomenon. A 1976 Library of Congress report points out that in 1967, shortly before war broke out in the Middle East, the then Secretary General of the United Nations, U Thant, was reported to have confided to friends that he considered UFO's the most important problem facing the United Nations next to the war in Vietnam. In fact, national interest was so acute in the 1960s that two committees of the House of Representatives did hold hearings. The first, in 1966, by the Armed Services Committee, did little more than mulch over the Air Force's involvement in the matter.

The second session, in 1968, by the Science and Astronautics Committee, opened the floor to various scientists and experts in the field who were under no official constraint to represent or perpetuate any specific views other than their own. The general consensus of the speakers was that UFO's definitely warranted further study. In his written statement Dr. Gary C. Henderson, Senior Research Scientist of Space Sciences at Fort Worth, Texas, remarked, "The public has been led to believe that everything has been done to either prove or disprove the existence of UFO's—rubbish!" He went on to point out:

> The current U.S. Air Force trend seems merely a statement that UFO's do not pose a threat to the security of the United States, and therefore warrant neither credence nor further concern. Similar words come from some of the few Congressmen with whom I have communicated. The discovery of Noah's Ark in Times Square would not necessarily pose a threat to national security either, but it would certainly be a find worthy of the most intensive investigation whether certain individuals accepted its existence or not.

"Are we making the same mistake the French Academy of Sciences made," asked Dr. Hynek, "when they dismissed stories of 'stones that fell from the sky'? Finally, however, meteorites were made respectable in the eyes of science."

Many of the myths surrounding the reporting of UFO sightings were attacked. Concerning the character of witnesses, Dr. Hynek stated that although some UFO's are reported by unreliable, unstable, and uneducated people, they are reported "in even greater numbers by reliable, stable, and educated people. The most articulate reports come from obviously intelligent observers; dullards rarely overcome their inherent inertia toward making written reports. . . . Some of the very best, most coherent reports have come from scientifically trained people." He also asserted that while some UFO reports may be generated by publicity, it is unwarranted to assert that this is the whole cause of high incidence of UFO reports. He added that other misconceptions are that UFO's "are never seen at close range, have never been detected on radar, and have never been recorded by scientific camera." The late

James E. McDonald, who was Senior Physicist at the Institute of Atmospheric Physics and Professor at the University of Arizona Department of Meteorology, commented on the much asked question of why astronomers never see UFO's.

> With almost two hundred times as many police, sheriffs' deputies, state troopers, et cetera, as there are professional astronomers, it is no surprise that many more UFO reports come from the law enforcement officers than from the astronomers. Furthermore, the notion that astronomers spend most of their time scanning the skies is quite incorrect; the average patrolman almost certainly does more random looking about than the average professional astronomer. Despite these considerations, there are on record many sightings from astronomers. . . .

As to physical evidence of UFO's, Dr. James A. Harder, Associate Professor of Civil Engineering at the University of California, quoted the case of the metallic fragments recovered by some fishermen in the town of Ubatuba in Brazil, after they had seen a flying disk explode. Analysis of the substance revealed it to be magnesium of an exceptionally high degree of purity, certainly, as Dr. Harder said, "far beyond the capacity of fishermen at Ubatuba to produce." He informed the committee that "such pure magnesium is indeed produced terrestrially in connection with Grignard reagents, and produced by the Dow Chemical Company, where magnesium is produced in greater purity actually than this." But he went on to point out that the alloys making up the .1 percent impurity are "very curious kinds of alloys from any terrestrial point of view."

In his prepared statement nuclear physicist Stanton T. Friedman acknowledged, "I have concluded that the Earth is being visited by intelligently controlled vehicles whose origin is extraterrestrial. This doesn't mean I know where they come from, why they are here, or how they operate."

He went on to speculate on various aspects of space travel. Regarding the feasibility of electromagnetic propulsion systems he stated,

> There is a body of technology which I have studied and which leads me to believe that an entirely new approach to high speed air and space propulsion could be developed using the interactions between magnetic and electric fields with electrically conducting fluids adjacent to the vehicles to produce thrust or lift and reduce or eliminate such other hypersonic flight problems as drag, sonic boom, heating, etc. . . .

His notation that "at Northwestern, turning on a magnet inside a simulated re-entry vehicle with a plasma around it resulted in a change in the color of the plasma and its location relative to the vehicle" is of particular interest since electromagnetic effects are frequently observed in association with the presence of UFO's, along with the fact that many observations suggest that what is being observed is a vehicle with a plasma region adjacent to it. This impression of a plasma region is given by the appearance of bright glows rather than color, changes in the color of the glow associated with velocity, luminous boundary layers and appearance on film of regions not seen by the naked eye. The well-known electromagnetic effects associated with UFO's include interference with the operation of automobile engines, radios, and headlights, interference with the operation of radio and television sets, compasses, magnetic speedometers, and power systems, and residual magnetism in metal objects, watches, and so forth. He reproached "non-believers" for their assumption that our technology is the ultimate—

> a presumption made by each generation of scientists in the last seventy-five years and proved wrong by the next generation of engineers and applied scientists. If there is

one thing to be learned from the history of science it is that there will be new and unpredictable discoveries comparable with, say, relativity, nuclear energy, the laser, solid state physics, high field superconductivity, etc. It is generally accepted that there are civilizations elsewhere which are much more advanced than are we. Look what technological progress we have made in the last one hundred years. Who can guess what we will accomplish in the next thousand years—or what others have accomplished in the thousand or million or billion year start they may have on us.

He quoted Max Planck's saying that new truths come to be accepted not because their opponents come to believe in them but because their opponents die and a new generation grows up that is accustomed to them. "Perhaps," he said, "this is what will happen with UFO's."

Dr. Harder claimed, "on the basis of the data and ordinary rules of evidence, as would be applied in civil or criminal courts, the physical reality of UFO's has been proved beyond a reasonable doubt." In support of the extraterrestrial hypothesis Dr. R. Leo Sprinkle, of the Division of Counseling and Testing at the University of Wyoming, declared, "I accept the hypothesis that the Earth is being surveyed by spacecraft which are controlled by representatives of an alien civilization or civilizations. I believe the 'spacecraft hypothesis' is the best hypothesis to account for the wide range of evidence of UFO phe-

nomena." Dr. Sprinkle's adjustment from scoffer to skeptic to unwilling believer came about initially as a result of two personal sightings of UFO's. Dr. McDonald concluded his remarks on the various hypotheses with the statement that "if the UFO's are not of extramundane origin, then I suspect that they will prove to be something very much more bizarre, something of perhaps even greater scientific interest than extraterrestrial devices."

During the hearings testimony and statements were presented by twelve scientists all together, who brought to light many case histories and relevant scientific data that had previously remained unpublicized. However, the purpose of the hearings was to serve as a forum, not to resolve the problem. Thus the absence of any national effort to deal with the situation continued.

· 30 ·

UFO'S AND THE LAW

In February, 1975, the *FBI Law Enforcement Bulletin* published an article dealing with UFO's, the first law enforcement publication to do so. The article recounted several spectacular UFO sightings by policemen and went on to describe the procedures that should be followed in future cases. The following October, *Spring 3100—The Magazine for Police Officers by Police Officers* followed up with an article entitled "Aerial Phenomena and the Police." It protests, ". . . can we continue to ignore it—pretend we don't see the lights and assume that the citizen witness is lying or crazy? The Police Department doesn't think so—and neither should you." Included in advice to police officers on how to handle reports is the caution, "Above all, do not ridicule the witness. A great deal of potential information (perhaps information that would help identify the UFO) is lost because an individual does not come forward through fear of being laughed at." Some photographs of UFO's generally accepted as legitimate are included and the writer concludes, "A professional approach will keep us from being swept up in a 'cop and saucer' tea party."

Following the two sightings in Enfield and publication of the *FBI Law Enforcement Bulletin* article, Enfield Chief of Police Walter J. Skower issued Special Order #75–20, instructing his men in the procedures to be followed in the case of future UFO sightings. In a statement submitted to the authors specifically for publication in this book, Chief Skower describes the problems faced by police in investigating reports of aerial phenomena:

> . . . These occurrences [Enfield sightings and UFO article in the *FBI Law Enforcement Bulletin*] prompted a rethinking of our traditional attitude toward such reports; where we once considered such sightings as frivolous or the result of overly stimulated imagination, we now realized that most of the reports were of a serious nature. In fact, most people were reluctant to make such reports since they felt they might be ridiculed or type-cast as persons with a mental problem.
>
> Though our Department does not have the scientific know-how or equipment to investigate or evaluate such reports, we also realized that we were the only local agency a concerned citizen could turn to.
>
> In an attempt to formulate a Department Policy, we contacted various State Agencies to find out what sort of response or investigative capability was available on that level. We found none. We spoke with several individuals in Federal Agencies having something to do with aviation and found that we could rely on very little cooperation or actual aid from them. Some individuals told us privately that their agencies had an unofficial or *quasi* official,

```
              ENFIELD POLICE DEPARTMENT

SPECIAL ORDER #75-20                    DATE: May 7, 1975

FROM: Walter J. Skower                  SUBJECT: U.F.O.'s
      Chief of Police


All reports of unidentified flying objects shall be fully investigated and a
case report number issued to each incident.

In addition to the regular case report form, a special report form titled
"Report on Unidentified Flying Object(s)" shall be made out as completely as
possible and attached to the original case. This report form has been
supplied to us by NICAP -- National Investigations Committee on Aerial
Phenomena. In any particular incident a form should be made out for every
individual making or involved in a sighting, including police officers.

If a continuing sighting of a U.F.O. is reported, effort should be made to
take police photos of the object. If this is possible, take photos from
as many angles as possible and try to include a point of reference in the
pictures, such as skyline, buildings, cars, trees, telephone poles, etc.

Most U.F.O. reports will be of a routine nature and investigation will
consist primarily of interviews of witnesses after the fact. If, however, any
unusual phenomena occur in addition to sightings, special investigation
should be conducted as quickly as possible.

Should there be any reports of landings, physical damage, or a significant
possibility of physical evidence, the scene will be safeguarded and physical
evidence accumulated promptly for laboratory testing. Disruption of any
power source is a significant factor.

This Department does not want to sensationalize reports of "Flying Saucers."
Therefore, news releases will be factual and incidents will not be blown out
of proportion by speculation.

Copies of "NICAP" reports will be sent to "NICAP" at 3535 University Blvd.,
West Kensington, Maryland 20795. To facilitate this procedure a copy of the
case report and "NICAP" reports will be forwarded to the Chief's office for
information and mailing.

If a major and corroborated UFO incident occurs which would allow for
gathering of physical evidence or the need for scientific investigators and/or
equipment, then NICAP (Tel: 301-949-1267) and the "Center for UFO Studies"
in Evanston, Illinois (for police use only) will be contacted immediately.
At such time inform them of the situation and, if they indicate an immediate
interest and wish to respond with personnel and/or equipment, they will be
given full cooperation. If such arrangement would require any unusual or pro-
longed deployment of Police personnel, then the Chief of Police or Police
Lieutenants will be notified.
```

Enfield Police Department Special Order #75–20

hands off policy, concerning UFO sightings and might even deny the existence of actual evidence if it in fact, existed.

After describing the satisfactory cooperation given by

NICAP and the Center for UFO Studies and his desire to maintain that contact, Chief Skower continues:

> At present, we are considering the establishment of a special unit within our Auxiliary Police Force which could be utilized to make a special investigation when we receive multiple sighting reports over a period of days. Except for initial investigations, regular officers do not have the time to themselves "stake out" or watch sections of the sky for protracted periods of time. The Auxiliaries, which are a sworn voluntary unit, would have the capability. We are prepared to make available to such a unit, photographic cameras and the Department's mobile video-tape camera.
>
> The Enfield Police Department is representative of the community, in that, not all officers take UFO reports seriously, but many do. All officers do feel they should be properly investigated. Management itself feels it is our duty to look into the matter as far as we can within our limited ability. Our training officer, Herbert Foy, an experienced and competent officer, was granted permission to become a NICAP regional investigator for the State of Connecticut. He performs this function on his own time at no cost to the community.
>
> Though most Police Departments are ill-equipped to conduct comprehensive aerial phenomena investigations, we feel it is our responsibility since other larger government agencies have shunned such responsibility and ignoring the reports does not make the problem go away. The people want to know what is going on and they have a right to some sort of answer.

Reaction by law enforcement officials to the July 4 sightings in Parsippany was equally strong. Within a few months Ernie was invited to speak at a conference, attended by local officials, police officers, and FBI agents, convened specifically to prepare a program of procedures to be followed upon future UFO sightings. As usual there was some frustration over past handling of the matter. Says John Fox, Sheriff of Morris County, "The Law Enforcement community can no longer push this problem aside. The Federal Government either is not interested, has given up, or is covering up the results of their investigations." He strongly urges, "This is not a law enforcement prerogative; since we are paid by the public, it is mandated—the public will expect us to respond within our capabilities to the report of a UFO. Not to respond or to be prepared, in my opinion, is next to nonfeasance of office." Deputy Chief Arthur Denny of the Parsippany–Troy Hills Police Department recalls the panic created in 1938 by Orson Welles's realistic broadcast of the H. G. Wells classic *War of the Worlds*. Thousands of people actually believed that Earth was being invaded by creatures from Mars. He is afraid that one day a UFO sighting might cause another such panic. Says Denny, "Police are the front line contact with the public and we must be capable of rendering assistance without creating fear or panic. When we ourselves can create this atmosphere, then and only then can we assist the people and the United States Government in learning some day what these aerial phenomena are all about."

PART

Six

HUMAN BEINGS AS
CELESTIAL PASSENGERS

ASTRONAUTS
AND UFO'S

"Considering the number of UFO sightings made by our space flight crews," says Al Chop, looking back at his days as Information Officer for NASA, "I think the government should consider a formal routine for investigation should our shuttle crews have another opportunity to make observations. At least they would be better prepared for reporting on the phenomena than during Mercury, Gemini, and Apollo, et cetera."

Much has been written about the sightings of UFO's by astronauts, yet controversy reigns. Les Gaver, Chief of the Audio Visual Branch of the Public Information Division at NASA, states,

My sixteen years as Chief of Audio Visual for NASA has placed me as editor of all the onboard film taken by our astronauts. It actually began with the MR 2 Mercury flight with Ham the chimpanzee. Of course with Ham it was a remote control sequence camera. Of all the

100,000 pictures taken by all the manned space flights I have never been convinced of the UFO theory. There have been a number of pictures where you see reflections, space junk, ice crystals, scratch marks on film, dust on film holders, lights on the ground, and other spacecraft such as the Agena stage and spent boosters that many researchers call UFO's. This is not the case. However, I must admit there are some frames taken by astronauts that are unexplainable. I place them in the category of space phenomena such as air glow, northern lights, aurora, etc.

Certainly the photographic evidence of UFO's sighted by astronauts and pilots is very poor in quality. One such case is that of a UFO spotted by Air Force Major Robert M. White and believed to be the same object captured on film by a movie camera mounted in the lower tail of his X-15 aircraft. The film showed an object of undetermined size and gray-white in color tumbling above and behind the X-15 as it climbed through 270,000 feet. NASA officials believe that the object may have been one of several ice particles flaking off the frosty sides of the research aircraft. Although it seems probable that this is the explanation, there was no means of proving this theory nor was there any way positively to identify the photographed object as the same one seen by Major White. However, a look at a frame from the film shows us an unspectacular white blob, typical of most NASA footage

of UFO's, although some are more interesting in that they appear to be in formation.

Astronaut Jim Irwin says of his fellow astronauts, "The guys have reported sightings of a lot of UFO's, but I don't think any of them would seriously say that they looked like extraterrestrial spacecraft." Still the subject of much debate is the object observed by Gemini 11 astronauts Gordon and Conrad during their sixteenth revolution on September 13, 1966. A transcript of a taped report of the sighting reads,

> We had a wingman flying wing on us going into sunset here off to my left. A large object that was tumbling at about 1 rps, and we flew. . . . we had him in sight, I say fairly close to us, I don't know, it could depend on how big he is, and I guess he could have been anything from our ELSS [extravehicular life support system] to something else. We took pictures of it.

Of the three photographs taken the second and third showed four distinct white blobs surrounded by a red-orange corona. The blobs are in a different arrangement in each picture, suggesting either individual motion of separate objects or some sort of rotation of a single large object in the intervals between the taking of the pictures. The Condon Report concluded that the photographs recorded multiple pieces of the Russian space launch vehicle Proton III. But the NORAD report on the Proton III lists only two pieces, satellite and booster. In an article in *Science and Mechanics* in June, 1969, Lloyd Mallan established that since the astronauts were facing southeast toward the sunset and away from the direction of Proton III, which was actually about four hundred kilometers behind them, it would have been impossible for them to have seen the Proton III through the tiny windows of the space capsule, which permitted only a narrow forward view. Moreover, he pointed out that Astronaut Gordon

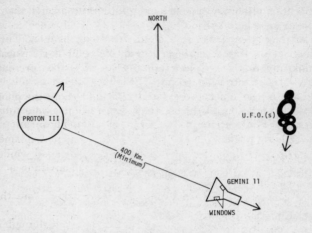

Diagram showing the positions of Proton III, Gemini 11, and UFO's witnessed by Astronauts Gordon and Conrad

had stated that when the object was first seen through their left window "it flew out in front of us and then we lost it when it sort of dropped down in front of us." The direction of the object or objects was opposite that of Proton III. Dr. Bruce Maccabee of the Naval Surface Weapons Center in Silver Spring, Maryland, goes on to demonstrate, in a paper prepared in 1975, several other inconsistencies in the Proton III identification. As a result of careful calculations he was able to prove that based on the distance of the Proton III from Gemini 11 the image sizes on the photographs are much larger than they should be, the image brightness much greater, and the relative motions of the individual blobs much greater than could be expected for relative motions between the satellite and its booster during the period (a minute or less) between pictures. Dr. Maccabee considers the possibility of the object or objects being trash but asserts that it could not have been trash from Gemini 11 since it was in a different orbit. He submits that the likelihood of a close encounter with trash in another orbit is statistically miniscule but not impossible. The object is presently listed by NASA as unidentified.

When we asked astronaut Jim McDivitt about the photographs he had taken of a UFO in space, which were subsequently released by NASA, he insisted, "Those are not the pictures that I took." The photographs, he explained, showed sun flares reflected on the multiple-paned window of his capsule, and, he said, "they weren't anything at all like what I saw."

"The photographs that you took," we asked, "are they available?"

"No," he answered, "I went back and looked through all the frames of all the photographs that were taken on that flight and there wasn't anything in there that looked like what I'd taken."

The possibility exists, he points out, that his camera never captured the image he was observing.

I just grabbed two cameras that were floating in the space craft right near me at the time. I snapped the pictures and—all this took place in just a matter of seconds—I never set the camera for the right F-stop, the right distance, the right speed, or anything else. I just grabbed it and pushed the button because that was the quickest thing I could do. Then the sun came across the window and I couldn't see through it any more. It was dirty. By the time I flew the space craft back to a position where the sun wasn't on the window, I couldn't see out any more. Since in those days we didn't number the film magazines, we couldn't go back and say which pack of film it was on. But I looked through each and every film that we had and it just didn't appear there at all. But there are a

Astronaut James McDivitt, who saw a UFO in space
(Courtesy NASA)

lot of photographs that are blank or overexposed or underexposed.

What did the object that he saw from his space capsule look like? "It was a white cylinder with a long, white, thin cylinder sticking out of it. It looked like a beer can with a pencil stuck in it, except that it was all white." A quiet, sincere man, McDivitt is completely openminded on the subject of UFO's. Both he and Erwin stress the difficulty of judging size and distance in space, which compounds the problem of identifying the millions of particles floating in space. We asked McDivitt if what he saw could have been a craft of some sort.

"I don't know," he said.

What did he think it was?

"I don't have any idea what it was. It could have been a beer can with a pencil in it!"

· 32 ·

IS IT ALL WORTH WHILE?

"Despite statements to the contrary," says Al Chop, "I feel the government (Air Force) continues to take an interest in the subject."

After all, they have the responsibility to safeguard the USA from anything in the sky. How can they wash out UFO's! I believe the government could have used the UFO reports to condition and educate the American public about space vehicles, probability of life throughout the universe, celestial mechanics, et cetera. Had they done this from the beginning, or even in the past ten years, I think the taxpayers would have given much better support to our own space program. It is to be regretted the way we downplay space today.

Colonel John Powers, former NASA Public Relations Officer, is even more outraged by the apathetic attitude toward the space program. When we informed him of our intention to bring out the fact that the space program has served a purpose and that we did not go to the moon primarily to prove that we could get there, he retorted, "Please don't use the past tense." He is, he admits, very touchy about the subject. He is distressed by the misinterpretation of Neil Armstrong's expressed concern that the spirit of Apollo had not prevailed.

> The man on the street understood that to be the "gung-ho, jump on a rocket boy, and go to the moon" attitude. That isn't what he was talking about at all. The spirit of Apollo and what was really demonstrated, apart from the technological accomplishment of actually landing on the moon, was that in this country, when we develop a consensus, which we did with Apollo, we can do anything we choose—but we must choose.

"We are literally on the threshold of a major scientific frontier," says Congressman Don Fuqua. "Our achievements in space exploration, as remarkable as they are, are only the beginning." The late Dr. Wernher von Braun contended that "future historians aren't going to remember the last half of this century for its inflation, wars, or Watergate. They'll remember it as the period when man left home for the first time." Congresswoman Millicent Fenwick also laments that "too many citizens are unaware of the tre-

mendous advantages that come from the space program to the general public." Space exploration is not merely a spectacular demonstration of man's technological ability to reach another celestial body and return. We need to search for new land, for new resources, and the utilization of space may be necessary for man's continued survival. Despite Congressman Fuqua's prediction that "the principal impact of space exploration will occur in the future," the number of down to Earth benefits it has already yielded are too many to be counted.

There are those who say, "Let's straighten out this planet before going out into space to mess that up too." But a moratorium on space projects is not going to solve existing problems here on Earth. On the contrary, technological reform has proved in the past to be the tool that helps bring about social reform. As an example, "the solution to world poverty," says Hugh Downs, the well-known television personality, "must still be found in a setting undergirded by scientific advance, which nearly always makes less expensive the means of enhancing life." Others fear that advanced technology breeds new problems of its own but, Downs points out, "we can be sure that shortly after the discovery of fire someone burned someone else's house down. If fire had been successfully outlawed until crime was eliminated, we would still be struggling with our morals from the viewpoint, temperament, and digestion of animals."

The most often heard remark during street interviews on radio and television following space exploits is, "What a waste of money!", reminiscent perhaps of what one might have heard in Spain in the 1490s: "Why are Ferdinand and Isabella giving all that money to that *loco* Columbus?" "But let's compare the billions," says Hugh Downs.

The space effort is currently budgeted at three and one half billion dollars a year—an amount the Department of

Health, Education and Welfare spends every nine days. The total cost of the Apollo project was less than twenty-five billion dollars spread over nine years. Economists estimate that every dollar spent on space will yield six dollars in genuine new wealth. Human benefits are almost uncountable because they crop up in unforeseen ways as the technology spreads into other industries.

NASA, while it was brilliant at developing space technology, was less than brilliant in letting the public know the true value of its achievements. To resolve the problem a group of dedicated business executives recently formed an independent, nonprofit organization, the National Space Institute,° now headed by Hugh Downs as president, following the death in June, 1977, of its chairman of the board, Dr. Wernher von Braun. The board of governors includes such notables as Senator Barry Goldwater, Dr. James A. Van Allen, Hugh O'Brian, Arthur C. Clarke, Bob Hope, John Johnson, Ambassador Shirley Temple Black, and Reverend Fulton J. Sheen. Membership is open to anyone for a nominal fee. The aim of NSI is not to propose priorities for the space program, but to insure that all viewpoints are heard so that informed decisions can be made, which then establish the size and priorities of our efforts in space. When NASA talks of hardware, NSI can talk of human values and long-range perspective, the serving of pressing problems and future needs. In that sense NSI is an advocate for the best that the space program can be.

In cooperation with the NSI a new space museum is being developed a mile from Disneyland in Anaheim, California. This site for the Space Park Museum was chosen since it is near enough to Disneyland for millions of visitors each year to plan to see the historic space

° The National Space Institute, 1911 N. Fort Meyer Drive, Suite 408, Arlington, Virginia 22209.

exhibits and learn about the benefits of the national space program.

What is it that NSI has to teach us? To list all the examples of the transfer of aerospace technology to non-aerospace use would be an encyclopedic task. Let us just consider a few interesting applications from different sectors of our technology.

Perhaps the most obvious benefits to mankind are those accrued through the continued use and development of the numerous artificial satellites that have been spinning around our blue planet for almost twenty years now. The workhorse machines of today, satellites serve an ever-increasing number of purposes, such as weather forecasting, communications, intercontinental television broadcasting, scientific data gathering, solar observation, prospecting and management of natural resources, determining forest resources, drought-prone areas, and sources of water pollution, forecasting crops, evaluating natural disasters, improving land use, and detecting disasters such as forest fires, tornadoes, and floods.

Good weather forecasting saves money. An accurate five-day forecast, toward which satellite technology is progressing, has been estimated to save up to 5.5 billion dollars yearly in the United States alone, and as much as 15 billion dollars for the entire world. The savings would be reflected in agriculture, construction, transportation, recreation, and other industries. The detection of forest fires and floods and the tracking, forecasting, and analysis of storms, tornadoes, and hurricanes helps save life and property. The use of satellites by geophysicists to measure continental drift and the movement of land along geologic faults may even supplement the developing technique of earthquake prediction. Meanwhile, improved communications through satellites have enabled ships and airplanes to find faster, safer routings around storms, ice, and other obstacles.

One of the myriad purposes of Landsats, or land surveying satellites, is to monitor fresh water and promote better utilization by observing large areas on a repetitive basis. For example, satellite pictures of snow accumulation and possible locations of subsurface water supplies in relation to cities, irrigated areas, and industrial developments make future planning more accurate and economical.

As the world's food demand rises, accurate forecasting of harvests becomes more and more vital. But these servants in space go a step further. They also watch for the conditions in which destructive insects breed. These prolific, hardy survivors destroy some 10 percent of all crops grown in the United States, causing between five and six billion dollars' worth of losses. Estimates place the weight of Earth's insect population in excess of that of its human inhabitants by a factor of twelve. Hundreds of millions of people throughout the world are stung and bitten each year by insects, with resultant disease, blindness, and death. As new generations of these pests develop immunity to insecticides, man must find new ways to combat this enemy, diminutive in size but colossal in force. One such method is an unusual form of birth control. The females of many insect species can mate only once in a lifetime. Satellites that yield continuous detailed reports on soil temperature, moisture, and vegetation coverage enable scientists to determine the insect's breeding patterns. At the right moment millions of male insects sterilized by exposure to radiation are distributed among the invading swarms. The females, mating mostly with the overwhelming hordes of sterile males, can produce no offspring.

Communications satellites have widened television coverage, extended education and medical care to remote regions, and even reduced the cost of overseas phone calls. The Intelsat, or International Telecommunications Satellite System, an organization of ninety-one nations, has brought the advantages of telecommunication to most of the world.

Today the system consists of more than 6000 telephone circuits among 110 Earth station antennas located in sixty-six countries, and it is growing with new launches of improved satellites each year.

The ATS-6 (Applications Technology Satellite) launched in May, 1974, has enabled physicians to conduct medical consultations in remote areas and brought high school and college courses to students in isolated Appalachian, Rocky Mountain, and Alaskan communities. A typical case is that of a seven-year-old girl in a tiny Alaskan village who had caught her hand in the wringer of an old-fashioned washing machine. A doctor several hundred miles away flipped a few switches and the badly frightened child appeared on the screen. "Hold up your sore hand," said the doctor. "Now hold up your other hand and let me see if you can wiggle your thumbs." Both could see each other. Not only was the doctor able to allay the little girl's fear, but he was also able to diagnose and treat her almost as if they were in the same room. He prescribed to the native nurse how to clean, bandage, and resplint the broken thumb.

In May, 1975, a year after its launch, the one-and-a-half-ton ATS-6 was moved eight thousand miles to serve the people of India. There, through cheap antennas and television sets, it dispensed agricultural information, animal husbandry instruction, and family planning programs to some five thousand villages and cities, most of which are otherwise inaccessible. India views satellite education as the only means to break the back of its widespread illiteracy. Eventually satellite television could give every classroom a window to the world, but current reductions in funding seem to be closing the door to that dream. Until that door is opened again, India and other Third World nations will suffer social, moral, and political deprivation for lack of space activity.

Probably the best-known space spinoff to health is the

cardiac pacemaker. Heart pacemakers were introduced in the 1950s to rehabilitate patients with complete heart block. The electronic pacemaker delivers small, regular electric shocks, which stimulate the heart muscles to contract at a normal, steady pace. The original devices had to be removed every twenty-two months in order to recharge the batteries. This repeated surgery involved a risk factor and cost the patient well over two thousand dollars for each operation. Now, through space technology, a new pacemaker has been created that does not have to be removed. Once a week the patient simply puts on a charger vest for an hour to recharge his pacemaker. The recharging is done through the skin. Nothing has to be put into the body. Since recharging is done so frequently, only one cell is required and the size of the pacemaker has been reduced by half and now weighs only two ounces. Another major breakthrough has been that it is no longer affected by microwave ovens or automobile ignitions, which sometimes used to stop the original models. To thousands of people in the United States and all over the world, this little device means the difference between life and death.

Statistics show the bridge between life and death to be crossed all too frequently as a result of the various means of transport we all use in our daily life. Here again space technology is helping to reduce the risk factor. One of the many ways in which highway safety is being increased is by the development of studless winter tires. The rubber of these tires is the same as that used on the tires of the "Rickshaw" used by astronauts Alan Shepard and Stuart Roosa to transport equipment on the moon in 1971. Conventional tires lose their pliability below freezing. The hard rubber begins to bounce, losing surface traction. Several states have banned studded tires because their traction on dry surfaces is poor and they destroy road surfaces. The new winter tires provide traction even in the coldest weather. After all, they remained pliable in lunar temperatures as low as 195 degrees below zero! The cords of this tire are also a space spinoff. They utilize a new fiber that is five times stronger than steel. Just three straps of this new fiber were needed to attach the first 2300-pound Viking lander to the parachute that lowered it to its historic touchdown on Martian soil on July 20, 1976.

Safer highways and airport runways are resulting from an extensive research program conducted by NASA on cutting grooves in runways to eliminate airplane skidding during rainy weather. Now sawed into highways, the grooves facilitate water runoff, improve contact between tire and surface, and reduce hydroplaning, a phenomenon created by a thin layer of water on the road surface that causes tires to slip. Wet highway accidents on grooved sections have been reduced by about 60 percent. New uses studied by NASA include pedestrian walks, playgrounds, sanitary concrete slabs in cattle ranches and dairy farms, loading docks, ramps, warehouse floors, and anywhere that men, animals, or machines can slip on wet surfaces.

Increased use of trains, particularly freight cars, and deferred maintenance of track are major factors in the enormous rise in train accidents. A Connecticut company, Automation Industries, developed a unique rail inspection device to help reduce the alarming figures. When NASA sought a fast, nondestructive way to inspect butt welds in aluminum alloys for spacecraft, Automation Industries developed for them a reliable ultrasonic device using multiple transducers. Called a "delta manipulator," it can detect lack of weld penetrations not readily seen in radiographs. They then adapted the ultrasonic equipment to a device that is contained in self-propelled railroad cars to check old track welds for deterioration, an inspection service that saves countless manhours. The company operates twenty-eight of the cars on United States rails and several in Australia, Europe, and Mexico. The cars move along at about 7 miles per hour, inspecting 160,000 miles of track annually for a hundred different railroads.

Of less frequent service but vital to those few who find themselves in need of it is the life raft. In 1959 NASA designed a life raft utilizing a radar-reflective material to assure that astronauts could be found if their returning spacecrafts were off course. Several companies attempted to design a commercial version, but it wasn't until a scientist named Robert Perchard developed his own improved version that it entered widespread use. Perchard had a personal reason. His son, a Coast Guard pilot, had crashed in Alaskan seas. By the time conventional radar searching located his life raft, it was too late. He had died of exposure. Perchard's new design incorporated a thermally insulated, radar-reflective canopy colored speckled orange for easier sighting. He made dozens of other improvements too, in both rafts and life preservers. A man floating with a life preserver utilizing the radar-reflective material can be sighted from an altitude of 6000 feet. Today the rafts and life preservers are carried by the world's navies, merchant marines, and pleasure aircraft and boats.

The idea of our world being taken over by the ultimate computer still remains in the realms of science fiction. But every day these incredible machines are making their presence felt more and more strongly. Getting through the weekend without cash because you forgot to go to the bank on Friday is no longer a problem. You make a quick trip to a nearby bank, slip your credit card into a slot in the wall, and the automatic machine spits out the money. The use of automated bank facilities, both to assist tellers and, in some cases, to do without them, is increasing rapidly due to the competition among banks in providing

greater customer convenience as a result of speedier transactions and eliminating almost all normal teller entry
errors. Credit authorization terminals and computerized
cash registers can now be seen in retail stores all over the
country. Average improvements of the credit authorization
terminals over nonautomated methods include a 95 percent
reduction in purchases on bad debt accounts, 75 percent reduction in fraudulent purchases, 20 percent cost
savings in payroll for authorization employees, and 33
percent reduction in telephone calls. The computerized
cash register terminals provide improved inventory control,
more accurate and faster sales transactions, more detailed
merchandising information, and better sales data for management analysis. These and other complicated systems
that have played a leading role in the nation's productivity
increase were spun off from one of the most complex computer systems in the world—the automatic checkout equipment devised for the manned missions to the moon, built
to integrate the extensive Apollo spacecraft procedures
from manufacture to launch.

Lately we have been made all too aware of a major factor
in the nation's economy: energy. NASA's involvement is
not only in the field of detecting fuel deposits. For some
time now we have been hearing about the construction
of the Alaska pipeline. As the oil makes its long journey
southward from Alaska's rich new fields, space technology
can be considered largely responsible. A major construction
problem in the arctic is posed by the seasonal freeze-thaw
cycle of the permafrost soil. Frost heaving, which can
raise structural piling by as much as eighteen inches in one
year, is followed by uneven settling during the summer
thaw. The enormous forces involved would literally tear
a pipeline apart, spewing hot oil over the countryside.
NASA developed heat pipes for cooling onboard electronic
packages used by Skylab and still used routinely by satel-

lites. The heat pipe system was adapted to solve the Alaskan permafrost problem. A sealed tube contains anhydrous ammonia, which has a boiling point of 25 degrees Fahrenheit. The ammonia evaporates as it soaks up heat from the 30 degrees Fahrenheit permafrost. The heated gas rises to the top of the pipe and dissipates the heat through a fin type radiator. Having condensed back to a liquid, the anhydrous ammonia returns to the bottom of the pipe and the cycle repeats itself continuously, never allowing heat above 25 degrees Fahrenheit to penetrate the permafrost. Thus heat pipes are totally automatic. They sense and respond to climatic conditions with no moving parts, require no external power, and never need adjustment or servicing. This truly revolutionary device will keep the ground frozen along the 798-mile pipeline, saving hundreds of millions of dollars and protecting the tundra environment.

Space spinoffs have resulted in many new products to improve the quality of our recreational activities. For the skiing enthusiast come electrically heated gloves and skiboots, adapted from spacesuit designs that kept astronauts warm or cool in the temperature extremes of the moon. Batteries worn inside the wrist of the glove or sealed in the sole of a skiboot are rechargeable hundreds of times. They operate a flexible resistance circuit, which is turned on periodically when the wearer wants to be warmer. The thermal gloves and boots also utilize space insulation materials and techniques. Unheated thermal gloves would be adequate as long as the insulation stays dry. The problem is that it does not. Moisture from without, or from perspiration, saturates conventional insulations. The monofilament open-mesh material used in lunar spacesuit boot liners is utilized to absorb the moisture.

Hands and feet now comfortable, the skier wants to see where he is going. Keeping ski goggles from fogging is just one of dozens of uses for the anti-fog coating developed to keep spacecraft windows clear before launch. The basic composition of the coating includes a liquid detergent, deionized water, and an oxygen-compatible, fire-resistant oil. Two thin coatings are applied to the glass or plastic surface and buffed lightly. This anti-fog coating can be used on all transparent surfaces such as eyeglasses, deep-sea diving masks, firefighters' face shields, and vehicle windows.

For the golfer composite materials used in many space structures have been adapted for lighter, more efficient golf clubs. The reinforced composites provide the combination of shaft rigidity and flexibility that provides maximum distance.

And for the more daring who seek to fulfill the age-old desire to emulate our feathered friends there are the flying trapeze-like kites that hang beneath colorful wings originally designed to recover spacecraft. Hang gliding is a rapidly growing sport. The wing is simple to control. Pulling back on the control bar allows you to pick up speed and at the same time lowers your altitude. Pushing forward slows your speed and levels you off. You push left to go right and vice versa. Birdmen can choose from prone, upright, or swing-seat harnesses in either kits or ready-to-fly gliders.

For those who wish to spend their recreation time in a more relaxed manner there is one of the most attractive theater-concert halls in the world. The University of Akron's performing arts hall is a cultural and architectural

triumph. It was constructed to accommodate concerts, ballet, opera, and theater productions. Although they are cultural relatives, they are, in fact, architectural opposites because the main hall has to shrink and expand to accommodate audiences as large as three thousand and as small as nine hundred. Movable ceilings were required not only to alter the size of the main hall, but also to regulate the volume and manipulate the acoustics. The most modern in the United States, the movable ceiling contains overhead hexagons that can be lowered in clusters either to exclude six hundred seats or to provide an additional fifteen hundred seats. Once the hall has been sound tuned, the various positions of this ingenious ceiling and related acoustic curtains may be called into play immediately by pushing buttons on a control console that has been programmed previously. Before an event a technician may condition the hall with the touch of a finger for chamber music, symphony, or theater. A simple, inexpensive tool devised in the space program was used to equalize tensions in the 150 cables of the ceiling, a tool originally developed to measure and adjust the cables of the elevators used at Cape Kennedy for lifting heavy spacecraft.

Transfers of aerospace technology to nonaerospace use are all around us and have more than paid for the cost of space exploration. During its two hundred years of existence this nation has grown from a country dependent on Europe for its machinery and technology to a position of dazzling preeminence. The space program has been a demonstration of that preeminence. But we cannot sit back and bask in past glory if we are to maintain that lead. Other countries are rising rapidly to challenge that position. A revitalized space investment is part of a larger emphasis on industrial growth that must be made if the United States is to retain its narrowing technological leadership.

Some day spinoff may acquire an even more expanded

meaning. It may include new crops hybridized with plants native to other planets. Or even knowledge transferred by communicating with intelligent life in other solar systems. So let us move on out into space in a continued search for the answers not only to the secrets of the universe but also to the secrets of living here on our own Earth.

· 33 ·

THE BLUE PLANET COMMUTERS

Human beings will be commuting back and forth from Earth to space on a weekly basis in the year 1980. No, this is not the prediction of Edgar Cayce or Jeane Dixon or any of the other well-known prophets of our time. This is one of the plans of the NASA space program. In 1973 the Skylab space station was launched. Three missions that year and the next proved that human beings can live and work in space for prolonged periods. In 1975 the joint United States–Soviet Apollo-Soyuz linkup provided experience in docking with dissimilar equipment and languages. The next step was to develop an economical, reusable vehicle that would enable us to establish a real working presence in space. That vehicle is the Space Shuttle. Now under construction, horizontal test flights are to begin in 1977, orbital test flights in 1979, and the complete vehicle is to be operational in 1980.

About the size of a DC-9 jet liner and capable of carrying a 65,000-pound payload, the shuttle will take off like a rocket and land like an airplane. In normal operations the personnel can vary from three to a maximum of seven. The basic crew consists of a pilot, co-pilot, and mission specialist. Accommodations are provided for both men and women. They will travel without spacesuits and undergo a maximum of three G-forces during launch and

Space Shuttle Orbiter being ferried
piggy-back-style by a 747 (*Courtesy NASA*)

reentry. Missions will last normally for about seven days, but when required will be extended for as long as thirty days.

The two shuttle launch and landing sites are located at Kennedy Space Center, Florida, and Vandenberg Air Force Base, California.

The shuttle will consist of a reusable orbiter, looking like a delta-winged airplane, mounted piggy-back at launch on a large expendable liquid propellant tank and two recoverable and reusable solid propellant rocket boosters. The orbiter consists of a cargo bay, sixty feet in length by fifteen feet in width, and three liquid fueled rocket engines. These engines are reusable and represent an advance from the previous state of the propulsion art.

At liftoff the three main engines in the orbiter and the

two solid rocket boosters are burned simultaneously, generating a total thrust of about 6.3 million pounds. After the shuttle has cleared the launcher tower, it performs a roll maneuver to the desired launch direction. At about 27 miles, two minutes into flight, the solid rocket boosters burn out and are detached. They descend by parachute to a predetermined site in the ocean. Here they are recovered, towed back to shore, refurbished, and reused on a subsequent flight. The orbiter and external tank continue powered ascent until about eight minutes from liftoff, when the orbiter main engines are shut down. The empty external tank, which provided liquid hydrogen and liquid oxygen to the engines, is jettisoned before orbit insertion and impacts in a remote ocean area. The orbiter then fires its orbital maneuvering system for a short period to achieve orbital insertion. Total time from liftoff to Earth orbit is ten minutes. The orbiter with its crew and payload remains in orbit to carry out its mission. Its mission completed, it then returns to Earth, landing on a conventional runway with a payload of up to 32,000 pounds.

The end of one mission marks the beginning of the next. There is no dead time between flights. In a 160-hour operation the payload is removed and the new one installed. The solid rocket boosters and the external tank are mounted and the shuttle is ready to depart again.

Already sixty to seventy shuttle missions per year are planned for the 1980s. One of the main tasks will be to place unmanned satellites into orbit and retrieve them later for repair, adjustment, updating, and reuse. When carrying a satellite to Earth orbital altitude, a specialist aboard the shuttle can check it out and validate its operation in the environment of space before committing it to its unattended operation. In the event that the satellite fails to perform as planned and on the spot repairs are inadequate, it can be returned to Earth for more extensive repairs. The same procedure is applicable to malfunction-

Above: Space Shuttle liftoff *(Courtesy NASA)*
Opposite: The various stages of a Space Shuttle mission

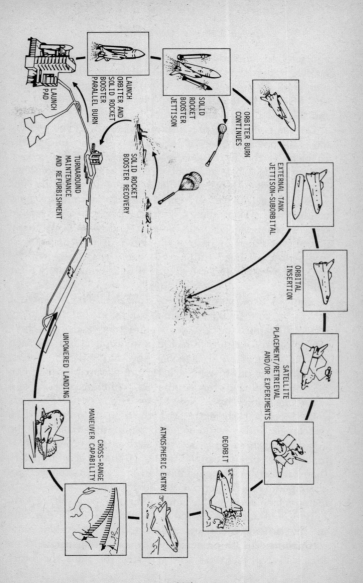

LAUNCH PAD

LAUNCH ORBITER AND SOLID ROCKET BOOSTER PARALLEL BURN

SOLID ROCKET BOOSTER JETTISON

ORBITER BURN CONTINUES

EXTERNAL TANK JETTISON-SUBORBITAL

ORBITAL INSERTION

SOLID ROCKET BOOSTER RECOVERY

TURNAROUND MAINTENANCE AND REFURBISHMENT

SATELLITE PLACEMENT/RETRIEVAL AND/OR EXPERIMENTS

UNPOWERED LANDING

DEORBIT

CROSS-RANGE MANEUVER CAPABILITY

ATMOSPHERIC ENTRY

ing satellites already in orbit. In a study of 131 past satellite failures 78 were related to launch problems. The remaining 53 failures were attributable to satellite anomalies. Most of these failures could have been avoided if the shuttle had been available.

On some flights a pressurized Spacelab, developed by nine European countries at their expense under the auspices of the European Space Agency, will be carried in the payload bay and will serve as a space laboratory. For the first time scientists and engineers who are not astronauts will have an opportunity to accompany and conduct their experiments in space. The research people who fly on Spacelab will be men and women of many nations, qualified in their fields and requiring only a few weeks of specialized training. In many cases they will be able to go home with the acquired data immediately after landing.

There will be many uses for Spacelab. The absence of gravity in an orbiting laboratory can be exploited in many ways. Ultrapure metals, semiconductors, and glass may be produced for research use and applications in such areas as electronics, laser technology, and optical products. Crystals of a purity and structure unobtainable on Earth may be produced for computers, communications, and other electronics uses. New types of composite materials with increased strength at high temperatures may be developed and new knowledge about materials may be acquired to advance processes used on the ground. Pharmaceutical serums can be made of much greater purity than on Earth, where convection and gravity effects are an impediment. Repetitive studies of metabolic and associated changes in plants and animals as a result of zero gravity will add to knowledge of medicine and contribute to the advancement of understanding of fundamental mechanisms in life processes. Astronomical instruments on Spacelab will help us study Earth, the sun, the other planets, and the universe. Through space science we will increase our knowledge of the basic processes in biology, chemistry, and physics. By looking outward from above Earth's atmosphere we can see things we cannot possibly see from the surface of our planet.

The shuttle will be capable of transporting payloads up to 500 miles in Earth orbit. However, there are many space missions that require higher orbits. To achieve these higher orbits a Space Tug is required. The Space Tug will be a reusable stage that will fit in the shuttle cargo bay with its payload and will be able to place and retrieve payloads in orbits beyond the capability of the shuttle. It will also be used to launch interplanetary spacecraft from orbit.

The Space Shuttle will reduce drastically the cost of space transportation because it will be the first reusable space vehicle. It will allow us to go into space routinely, with no tremendous effort and at very short notice. It will benefit users throughout the world and will open up new roads of opportunity that are far beyond our capabilities today. Through its promotion of aerospace technology the Space Shuttle will put us on the path to the future.

· 34 ·

MIGRATION TO SPACE

Dr. O'Neill is already informally recruiting for his first space colony of only 10,000 people, to be in place by 1990. We should begin recruiting for his 1990 beachhead and our 2000 city now. If interested contact me. Charles "Ed" Tandy, Prometheus Society, 102 Morris Drive, Laurel, Maryland 20810.

This was printed in the December 1975 issue of the newsletter of an international organization called the L-5 Society. It was not part of a science fiction story, nor was it a joke.

The L-5 Society, headquartered at 1620 N. Park, Tucson, Arizona, was established as a forum for all those interested in participation in the design and planning of new lands in space. It was named after a place in space where the first habitat is to be constructed. The long-term goal of the society is to disband in a mass meeting at L5.

The site was first discovered back in 1772 by the French astronomer Joseph Louis Lagrange. He found that there are five points along the same orbital path as the moon where the gravitational and centrifugal forces of Earth and the moon cancel each other out. Any object within one of these vast, roughly spherical areas would remain there, orbiting around Earth. They are known as the Lagrangian Libration Points and are numbered one through five. L1, L2, and L3 are not reliable because an object once pushed out of place would continue to drift away. But if anything should happen to push an object out of position at either L4 or L5, it would promptly move back, swinging or librating as it did so. L4, which lies ahead of the moon on its orbital path, and L5, which lies behind the moon on its orbital path, are each at a distance from the moon equal to that between the moon and Earth. These two points are a perfect location for the building of artificial habitats, where, like the moon, they would never be cut off from sunlight by Earth's shadow and where they could maintain a stable orbit without the need for any expenditure of energy.

Dr. Gerard K. O'Neill, a boyish-faced man with a sixties' Beatle haircut, is the father of this brainchild. Professor of physics at Princeton University, he gave birth to the idea when he posed the question to a special seminar of freshman physics students, "Is the surface of a planet

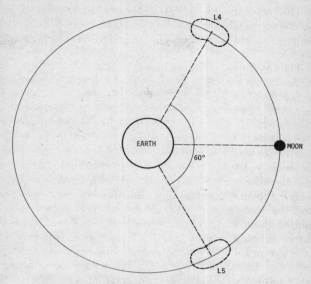

Diagram showing positions of L4 and L5 in
relation to the earth and moon (*Courtesy NASA*)

really the right place for an expanding technological
civilization?" The project grew and is now under the
sponsorship of the Polytechnic Institute of New York
and NASA.

Descriptions of the exterior of the space habitats bring
to mind the Starship *Enterprise* of the television series
"Star Trek," or the space station in the motion picture
2001: A Space Odyssey. To sustain conditions such as
earthlike gravity, normal day and night cycles, natural
sunlight, efficient use of solar power and of materials, the
design calls for a pair of cylinders, each sixteen miles long
and four miles wide, tethered together by tension cables
about fifty miles apart to ensure precise orientation in

space, and each counterrotating to cancel out any gyro-scopic effect the other might produce, so that they always remain pointed endwise toward the sun. Their rotation rate is once every two minutes, generating a centrifugal force that simulates gravity on the inner surfaces. Each cylinder is divided into six alternating strips of land area and blue-tinted window area. The length of each day can be controlled by the three huge rectangular mirrors that rotate with the cylinder and reflect the sun through the windows into the interior, providing light and heat and making the sun itself visible to the inhabitants as its reflection traverses the mirrors in an apparent dawn to dusk cycle. By changing the length of each day, the mirrors can create seasonal climates, and O'Neill suggests having winter in one cylinder while it is summer in the other. On the end cap nearest the sun is a solar power station consisting of paraboloidal mirrors that focus the heat on boiler tubes, which in turn energize conventional steam-turbine electric generators to provide the com-munity with a capability of ten times the power per person now used on Earth.

At the same end of the cylinder is a huge ring of non-rotating containers or pods in which crops can be grown under the enhanced conditions of continuous sunlight and without the hindrance of gravity. Each pod has its own separate environment, which can be adjusted to suit the particular crop it is to grow. Because there is no attempt to simulate any sort of earthlike appearance within these pods, they might sound like one of man's most unnatural inventions to date. Yet they could prove to be one of the most ecological methods of growing food. No insecticides or pesticides are needed for the growth of seeds in this sterile, isolated environment, and even if some infectious organism were to develop, its evolution time would be long, and resterilization of a contaminated pod could be effected easily by heating. The inhabitants of a cylinder

would not be limited in their choice of fruits and vege-
tables by seasonal dictates and everything could be eaten
fresh since it would be grown only twenty miles away.

While the unearthly, machinelike appearance of the
exterior of such a habitat might be unappealing to many
people, the inside is a different story. Renderings by artist
Don Davis show us a landscape of rolling hills, lush,
verdant valleys, crystal-clear streams and lakes, parklands,
and forests, stretching out under a blue sky sprinkled with
puffy white clouds. In this haven for bird, fish, and animal
species endangered on Earth by agricultural and industrial
chemical residues, man, too, may find this to be an ecological paradise. His senses will not be assaulted by a daily
barrage of roaring traffic, stifling smog, industrial pollution, and harsh extremes of temperature. His environment
will be designed essentially for his comfort and pleasure.
For housing O'Neill has suggested small apartment buildings against the endcaps with spacious rooms and wide
terraces overlooking the fields and woodlands. But any
architectural style could be followed, from baroque to
simple, from oriental to Scandinavian. The only forms of
transport needed to traverse the short interior distances
would be non-fuel-burning vehicles such as small electric
cars and bicycles. Individual heating systems would be
unnecessary since the unit would be heated as a whole
by solar energy. The climate itself would be controlled
to suit the inhabitants, even to the extent that the real
clouds in the sky could rain on them now and then.

Enjoying an uncrowded life-style, the inhabitants will
have at their fingertips all the usual forms of recreation
such as swimming and sailing in the lakes and rivers,
sunbathing on the shores, hiking in the woods, skiing, and
mountain climbing. But the sports that bring one to the
higher altitudes will involve some unearthly qualities.
The mountain climber will find his backpack becoming
lighter as he nears the mountain peaks, for the artificial

Above: Double cylinder space habitat, with
population capacity of up to several million *(Courtesy NASA)*
Below: Interior of the cylindrical space habitat, showing
the three land strips and the three windows with the sun
reflected through the upper window while Earth and the moon
are visible through the window on the left *(Courtesy NASA)*

gravity decreases as one gets closer to the central axis of the cylinder. Highboard divers at mountainside swimming pools might find themselves floating rather than plunging toward the water. And at the highest peaks people may truly emulate the birds with their own manmade wings. One wonders, however, how the birds themselves will cope with the bewilderment of floating effortlessly at times, only to have to work hard again as they reach different parts of the sky.

To visit friends and business associates in a twin cylinder requires only nine minutes of traveling time. An engineless vehicle unlocks from the surface of one revolving cylinder, is flipped into space by the centrifugal force at a speed of about 400 miles per hour, and locks into the other revolving cylinder at zero relative velocity. Later, tourism between the various habitats would be inexpensive and simple since there is no gravity to overcome. Low cost recreation vehicles consisting of well-furnished, pressurized shells with recirculating atmospheres could be used by families and by individuals to travel to other communities of diverse cultures and languages.

Obviously, the purpose of building space habitats is not to create a hedonistic paradise. There will be work to be done. One of the principal industries will be the manufacture of other habitats. Fortunately, though, the horrors of manufacturing will be removed to points outside the habitats where the vacuum and weightlessness of open space facilitate heavy industry and solar power provides it with unlimited energy for recycling. Some of the external pods designed for agriculture could be used for other industrial purposes, such as automated factories, laboratories, observatories, and even noisy or polluting sports such as auto racing.

One of the most outstanding aspects of building space habitats is the direct financial benefits they will return to Earth, the greatest being the efficient, inexpensive provision of solar power to our planet. One of our most oppressing problems today is the high cost, limited supply, and unpleasant side effects of our energy sources. Coal mining is hazardous to miners, strip mining ravages our countryside, and coal itself is an extremely dirty form of energy. Oil, also a pollutant and also heading toward depletion, has become a political tool. Nuclear energy produces radioactive wastes and involves risk to enormous portions of the population. While solar energy does not have these potentially dangerous characteristics, there are two obvious obstacles to harnessing it here on Earth. First, availability is limited by the day-night cycle, seasonal variation of the day length, atmospheric absorption, and cloud cover. Second, the collection and conversion apparatus requires vast areas of open, uninhabited land and involves huge capital investment. With habitats orbiting in space the obvious solution is for the inhabitants of those bases to build cheap solar satellite power stations, which would be placed in geosynchronous orbit above Earth to gather sunlight twenty-four hours a day. The power stations would convert the sunlight into microwave energy diffuse enough to satisfy stringent environmental requirements and beam it down to a receiving station on Earth, which would reconvert it to electricity. The cost would be a tenth of what it might be if such power stations were built on Earth and launched into space and the amount of land to be devoted to microwave reception would be as little as 5 percent of that required for direct solar energy reception. It is feasible that the solar satellite power stations could beam down enough power via microwave relay to supply the energy needs of the entire Earth in the year 2000, thus putting an end to starvation and poverty.

The building of habitats in space might not be feasible if the materials were to be obtained from Earth because of the prohibitive launch costs. However, only 2 percent of the materials for the initial structure will come from

Earth. The remaining 98 percent will be taken from the moon. Not only will it yield an abundant supply of substances such as aluminum, glass, concrete, soil, and oxygen, but lifting the materials off the moon will require only a twentieth the energy needed to lift them off Earth because the moon has such a weak gravitational pull. The strip-mined material will be launched by means of a unique device called the Transport Linear Accelerator, or TLA, which uses electromagnetic solar power to accelerate buckets of compacted ore along a six-mile course until they reach the low escape speed required. Deceleration of the bucket then releases the payload so that it is catapulted into space toward the construction site where it is scooped up by waiting pick-up vehicles. The excavation left on the moon after the removal of the materials for the first community would be a mere seven yards deep and about two hundred yards long and wide.

The most important element lunar material lacks is hydrogen, an essential component of water. Fortunately, Earth has plenty of hydrogen to spare since there is an oversupply. In fact, if the Antarctic and Arctic ice caps were ever to melt, the ocean level would probably rise two hundred feet, submerging much of Earth's most densely populated coastal plains. Thus while 89 percent of the mass of needed water would be obtained from the plentiful lunar oxides, 11 percent of the water mass would have to be transported from Earth in the form of liquid hydrogen. This, and the other materials making up Earth's 2 percent contribution to the construction supplies, will be ferried to L5 in a modified version of the Space Shuttle.

After construction of the first or second habitat, mining of the asteroid belt could commence. The asteroids are composed mainly of iron and nickel and also contain hydrogen, nitrogen, and carbon, thus eliminating the need to import these elements from Earth. The material of the asteroids would suffice for the construction of a total area

Model I space habitat *(Courtesy NASA)*

three thousand times that of Earth, and even if we were to be so industrious as to use them up within the next five hundred years, we could spend those years obtaining materials from the moons of the outer planets. It is hard to speculate beyond that point, but perhaps by then man's explorations will have reached out to another solar system.

Two models have been designed as small preparation habitats to be completed within ten years of commencement of the project and whose purpose will also be to test the technology involved so that any bugs can be weeded out before building the large habitats. Model I will be a mile long and about two hundred yards wide with a population of only ten thousand. The cost of this initial prototype will be comparable to that of the Apollo project. Economic payoff, however, will come within a few years as products and power produced make it financially self-supporting. Model II will have a larger population of one to two hundred thousand but with cost levels about the same. The large habitats to be constructed after Models I and II will be sixteen miles long by four miles wide and will each support a population of up to several million. In a bootstrap process each colony would help build the next at tapering costs. With access to unlimited solar power, the convenience of zero gravity for production and transportation, abundance of asteroidal materials, and the vast construction area available, it might not be long before billions of people are living out in space.

This would be the first space program where virtually anyone who wants to can take an active part in the adventure and, as with the colonization of the Americas, the space colonies would probably evolve toward independent government. With the efficiency of carrying on heavy industry in space Earth itself might become a beautiful wildlife preserve, a historical tourist haven for vacationing colonists. And the pioneer who might want to go out in search of greater adventure could build his own small

Interior of space habitat at dusk *(Courtesy NASA)*

vehicle, set out with his family and the basic requirements for agriculture and mining, and homestead an asteroid. Again, the lack of gravity makes this less expensive and less dangerous than a similar venture on Earth, for should anything go wrong with his craft, he could stop and fix it or radio to the nearest space habitat for help.

Accustomed as we are to living on the surface of a globe, the idea of moving to a manmade structure out in space might make us feel a little insecure. Yet Earth, too, is merely an object in space circling another celestial body, just as O'Neill's habitats would be orbiting Earth. The actual dangers involved are remarkably less awesome than they might seem at first consideration. The inhabitants of a space habitat will be protected from cosmic rays by the depth of the atmosphere, the soil, and the steel structure supporting the cylinders. As for meteor strikes, small meteors could only scratch and graze the exterior surface, while a meteorite large enough to cause any real damage is so rare that the chances of one striking a colony are once in a million years. Even then, there would be adequate time for repairs or evacuation. Some estimates place the leakdown time resulting from a hole the size of a normal window opening to be as long as three hundred years. Compared to all the dangers we face on Earth in the form of earthquakes, volcanic eruptions, hurricanes, and meteorite strikes, these hazards cannot be considered frightening.

So as we are approaching the limits of our Earth's storehouse and our environment takes on the aspect of a graveyard, it is time to cash in on the space technology that has already been pioneered and to reach out to new lands as our ancestors did before us. While no man can create Utopia, it is important to consider the new sense of hope and the creative and motivational stimulus that the move into space could inspire in mankind. It is almost certain that further work will uncover numerous technological and biological problems but we have become used to solving such problems in the course of our technological ventures in the past and with the uncovering of new problems comes the uncovering of new technological possibilities. As we clean up our fragile biosphere and attempt to restore Earth to its original condition of pristine beauty, we can continue the industrial revolution out in space, a process that has already brought comfort and freedom to a portion of the human race and that now perhaps can yield new wealth for all. It seems almost certain that other more advanced civilizations will not have confined themselves to the surfaces of their planets. We can now join those celestial passengers and seek our future in the pathless realms of space.

Some other books published by Penguin
are described on the following pages.

THE LOCH NESS STORY

Nicholas Witchell

During the summer of 1975 a large animal, moving about in the murky waters of Loch Ness, swam across the path of highly sensitive underwater camera apparatus. Scientists rushed the film to the United States under the strictest security, and the results of their astonishing findings are published in *The Loch Ness Story*. The legend of Nessie has grown up over fourteen hundred years, capturing the imagination of the world. Nicholas Witchell gives a careful, historical account of all the sightings and descriptions, together with photographs taken by amateurs and scientists as they watched on the shores; he relates the story of the many attempts to make the loch reveal its strange secret. "An excellent and lucid account"—Gerald Durrell in the Introduction.

SECRETS OF THE STONES
The Story of Astro-archaeology

John Michell

Have we at last uncovered the meaning of
Stonehenge and other enigmatic structures
built before the dawn of history? By careful surveys of megalithic sites from Brittany
to the Orkney Islands, a Scottish engineer
named Alexander Thom has recently shown
that these ancient earthworks are amazingly
accurate stations for observing the stars.
Conclusions similar to Thom's had been
reached before but had always been dismissed as impossible, since prehistoric peo-
ples were believed to have been too
benighted to comprehend astronomy. In
this volume John Michell traces the progress
of the astro-archaeological theory from the
eighteenth century to the present, when it
is virtually irrefutable. His is an astounding
narrative, for it reveals a prehistoric science
so advanced that its achievements can be
evaluated only in the light of our own.

THE MOON BOOK

Bevan M. French

How old is the moon? What is it made of? How was it formed? Is there life on the moon? Since 1969 twelve men have walked upon the surface of the moon and gained firsthand knowledge of earth's mysterious satellite. In less than a decade the Apollo Program has changed this heavenly body from an unknown and unreachable object into a familiar world. Bevan M. French brings this world to earthbound readers as he discusses man's early ideas about the moon and surveys the history of lunar exploration and the scientific findings of the Apollo Program. He examines current explanations for the earth-moon system and suggests that lunar exploration may also supply the key questions about the earth's early history and the origin of the universe itself.